MODEL

A STARTUP STORYBOOK

JEREMIAH MARBLE & DONA SARKAR

Published by Origin Stories 2019

Copyright © 2019 Jeremiah Marble & Dona Sarkar

www.model47.com

Disclaimer
Every effort has been made to ensure that this book is free from error or omissions. Information provided is of general nature only and should not be considered legal or financial advice. The intent is to offer a variety of information to the reader. However, the author, publisher, editor or their agents or representatives shall not accept responsibility for any loss or inconvenience caused to a person or organisation relying on this information.

Book formatting by Victor Marcos

ISBN:
978-1-79172961-5

Dedicated to our 46 entrepreneurs in Nigeria, East Africa and Europe.
Thank you for not doing the "safe" job.

The Journey Ahead

ORIGIN STORY

Like all great things, it started with a story.

We first heard it during a power outage in Lagos, Nigeria. The two of us and our crew were settled on the sixth floor of the Co-Creation Hub building — a startup incubator in the Yaba neighborhood fondly known as "Yabacon Valley."

Those who had been wise enough (aka not the two of us) to keep their laptops plugged into the power supply before the outage were working. Jeremiah and Dona had no power on their laptops, so instead were nagging the local startup founders to share stories of Nigerian culture.

As legend goes, a long time ago twins were born — Taiwo and Kehinde (pronounced *kay-en-day*). Taiwo (meaning "tastes the world first" in the *Yoruba* language) was the the eldest; the valiant one. Bravely, he emerged first into the world to look around. It was only after Taiwo had surveyed the new territory — legend tells us — would wise Kehinde (meaning "he who lags behind") sally forth. Kehinde wanted to ensure his sibling's experience was promising before heading out.

Everyone in Lagos wanted to tell us this story — reckless taxi drivers, driven startup founders, staid business leaders and rowdy bartenders. We learned that in Yoruba culture, most parents of twins (whether male or female) name their kids Taiwo and Kehinde — the order of their birth is important. The locals told us Nigerian culture thinks highly of prudent Kehinde over impetuous Taiwo. Culture favored his simple approach — wait and see, ensure everything's safe, and then act.

We found it fascinating, that the role of Kehinde would be the one preferred. The more we got to know Nigeria — and the continent of Africa as a whole, in fact — the more we would discover that adventurous Taiwo would be an example to uphold. This is a land of *hustle*.

The Nigerians and East Africans we met — living in Africa and abroad — aren't sitting around waiting for *things to happen*. They are a people who *happen to things*.

The book you're holding in your hands, Model 47, is a testament to all the Taiwos; all the entrepreneurs we've met all over the world. Each of them put aside their worries and "imposter syndrome" to give their idea the chance it deserves. We've been fortunate enough to work side-by-side with these driven, talented people. They are people like you.

We dedicate this book to you, Taiwo. You, the aspiring entrepreneur. You bring something important to your idea. It's not just your idea you contribute to that company in your mind you've been wanting to establish. Of course, your idea will grow. It will rush from that sudden flash of insight while you're on the bus, into a sloppy sketch you scribble onto a slightly greasy napkin as you grab that coffee. Your idea will crawl from that first rushed email you send to your friend into a full-fledged systems diagram. It will move along both slowly and quickly. It will constantly evolve. As time passes, you'll wear down its rough edges; you'll etch deeply into the details; you'll breathe its spark into a small flame. We'd describe the process as nothing short of magical, but we know you'll often feel that entrepreneurship is harried, scary and a slog.

Despite that, as the idea grows and evolves, it will absorb parts of you — it has to. Your idea isn't just an idea, stark on a blank page. It's colored by you — who you are, what you believe in, what scares you, what fills you with energy at daybreak. Your idea, your solution, and (we hope) your product — will be infused with you; with your love, your passion, your expertise. With your heartbreak and triumph. With your grit.

Each entrepreneur we've met is or becomes an expert in *something*. We've profiled their stories on our website Model47.com — feel free to reach out to them. They can relate to the journey you're on and understand it 100%. Rosine Mwiseneza is an expert in the Internet of Things (IoT) and solar energy. Andres Korin is an expert in risk analysis and financial restructuring. Olayinka (Yinka) Olanrewaju is an expert trial lawyer and orator, who will one day become the President of Nigeria. They didn't gain their knowledge in a classroom at a fancy university, but rather through years of experience. Frequently, entrepreneurs like you glimpse a market opportunity — or even a complex but important problem no one else is tackling; something that you experience in daily life — and that's the moment you step into that gap.

Paula Aliu didn't start out as an expert in young adult psychology. She learned the field as quickly as she could after her friend, who struggled with depression, committed suicide. Ange Uwambajimana learned about hardware design to solve a problem with IV drips because of an incident that nearly killed her brother.

Sometimes your insight comes from a joyful place. Leah Otieno, a matchmaker who brings people who love unique fashion and Kenyan tailors together wants to create jobs for artisans in her country. Daniel Isijola, an artist with astonishing talent, wanted to share the characters of his beloved Nollywood films with a wider audience (and help teach literacy at the same time). Kelechi Odoemena and his partner Kido Chukwunweike wanted an easier method of preparing the cowpeas that go into delicious traditional Nigerian meals such as moi-moi, akara and gbegiri, enabling Nigerian families to have more time for the important things in their lives rather than cooking meals.

Of course, these entrepreneurs we've met all around the world are also human. While they're blessed with strengths, they're also cursed with frailty, insecurity and flaws. Even the most talented of founders bring to their companies — along with their areas of expertise — areas in which they're less adept. Initially, Dr. Moses steered clear of marketing. Rosine shied away from public speaking. Andres outsourced much of his tech. Ange avoided financial modeling. To be honest, we're yet to find something Leah's not amazing at.

You know something else? Even though these entrepreneurs weren't expert *in everything, from the very beginning* they were all willing to roll up their sleeves and learn. In those areas where they lacked expertise, they made friends with those people who *were* experts.

They knew that one of the most important traits of a
successful founder is the ability to KEEP GETTING UP
and to KEEP GOING, even when the days get tough.

They believed in their ideas. They believed in themselves. They believed that they could learn the skills along the way; skills they'd need to establish and grow their businesses.

Just like Taiwo would, in the legend.

So, Model 47 is for Taiwos like them. Taiwos like you.

The story of Model 47 starts with the meeting of two battle-worn engineers who come from very different backgrounds, eventually becoming friends during an honest and vulnerable conversation.

Dona Sarkar calls herself an expert at failure. Though born in Kathmandu, Nepal, she grew up in one of the poorest neighborhoods in Detroit, Michigan. Her immigrant parents worked full-time jobs while going to school at night. Longing to become a non-starving artist, Dona sought a Computer Science (CS) degree in college; never having written a line of code in her life. Of course, she failed her first CS class. Dona didn't just get an embarrassing B-. She actually failed; as in received an "E" and got no credit for the course. She didn't give up, though. Four years (and several "E"s) later, she graduated with a hard-earned CS degree. She continued to struggle as a determined young woman in the alpha nerdy male-dominated tech world during an economic downturn. She started writing novels on the side so she could create fictional characters of people who made fun of her — and then kill those characters off (sorry, Fred). Five of her novels were rejected by every publishing house in New York before her sixth one finally hit the shelves at the local bookstore. She attended part-time fashion school to learn design skills and make her own clothes. While there, she accidentally chopped off a big chunk of her own hair, sewed her fingers together and bled all over her prized fabric — she tracked her progress by the number of disasters on her projects. Slowly, the disaster count lowered from the hundreds to the single digits. Her policy is to try everything five times — always succeeding on the fifth try. Doing the thing AGAIN is the name of her game.

Today, aside from her day job as a seasoned software engineering leader at Microsoft, Dona has built several independent businesses from scratch which solve problems she sees in the world. She's the founder and head designer of Prima Dona, an ethical fashion line that creates jobs for tailors in emerging markets. She's the co-founder of Fibonacci Sequins, a fashion blog showcasing the interesting and diverse people within STEM fields. She's written and published a series of Young Adult fiction books targeted at people who don't quite "fit in" and, most recently, career books for professionals to elevate their career.

Jeremiah Marble was born in Western Massachusetts. Growing up, he lived in Mt. Airy, North Carolina; Marietta, Georgia, and Melbourne, Florida as his family followed his father's sales regions whenever he'd be relocated. Jeremiah learned the value of hard work and frugality early on, first mowing lawns then later bagging groceries during high school, thereafter as a janitor and night watchman.

Despite dreams of becoming a poet, he realized art wouldn't pay off his college loans. After completing a Computer Science degree and launching a few failed startups, he began consulting on Wall Street. Jeremiah stared helplessly up at the September 11, 2001 terrorist attacks that destroyed his office on the 62nd floor of World Trade Center Tower 2. At that moment, he realized how much more he needed to do with his time on earth. He switched fields and changed continents.

For a decade, Jeremiah worked in international development. He served in the Dominican Republic with the Peace Corps, was Director of Operations for a social enterprise in Cambodia and Laos, was a Fulbright Scholar studying climate change in Costa Rica, and then worked at the United Nations in Paris leading educational software projects in Africa and Asia.

Eventually, he returned to the United States. After finishing business school, he joined Microsoft because of its mission — to empower EVERY person and organization on the planet to achieve more. He was determined to help create tech for the emerging markets in which he'd spent the previous decade.

We love a good side-hustle around here; and Jeremiah's is a consulting business called Boxes and Foxes, where he helps entrepreneurs understand their business models and whether it's a hobby, a business or a non-profit.

By chance, one fine day the two of us were thrown together to be partners on the Windows Insider Program at Microsoft. Windows Insiders form a global community of over 16 million people in every country in the world — all seeking to use their technical skills to create value in the world. Our first conversation focused on the overwhelming desire we both had to share what we'd learned throughout the years, so those who don't come from a privileged background aren't left behind. We both have incredibly different upbringings and experiences, yet we have learned similar lessons.

Together, we created the idea of a fellowship program where we could learn first-hand about the tech and business needs of entrepreneurs all over the world (this would help us influence product teams at Microsoft to build products for 7.6 billion people) and we could share what we'd learned in return. We pitched the idea to our friend and mentor, Engineering Director Bambo Sofola — the son of a sociologist and one of Africa's first female playwrights. As we described our goals for the fellowship, it became abundantly clear that Lagos, Nigeria was where we would start. We would come to learn that 80% of Nigerians identified entrepreneurship as something they did or planned to do in future.

We coerced, ahem, *recruited* a crew of like-minded volunteers who also didn't mind the major "imposter syndrome" we were all feeling.

Then we got on a plane.

And here we all were during one of the regular rolling blackouts in Lagos, Nigeria, the two of us and our crew — Bambo, Raji, Guille, Fernie, LaSean, Dara and Tom from Seattle; and Shina, Kendra, and Paula from Nigeria.

For this inaugural program, we partnered with the incubator and community center Co-Creation Hub (CCHub) for their local expertise and deep relationships. From more than 5,000 applicants, we had together selected a cohort of 25 entrepreneurs with amazing ideas to make Nigeria an even better place. Our goal was to work side-by-side with these fellows to launch 25 viable businesses.

We initiated the fellowship with a week-long bootcamp to kick start the 25 ideas, as well as start the process of providing ongoing tech and strategic mentorship for a period of six months.

On the morning of November 14, 2016, all 25 strangers walked into CCHub — each with a story, an idea, and pure enthusiasm to build their business. Among them was Dr. Moses Keller, a young doctor trying to save women from dying in childbirth. Paula Aliu was looking to help troubled youth get access to mental health services. Kelechi Odoemena was seeking to free up time for Nigerian families. Olayinka Olanrewaju was attempting to help more Nigerian law students pass the bar exam. Bem Asen wanted to make sure that elderly people, like his father, who found themselves suddenly unemployed, were able to find work again.

We kicked off the bootcamp with introductions and goals, despite the continued major "imposter syndrome" EVERY person in the room was feeling — especially us two.

Then we asked the hard questions: "Who are you building this for? What's their name? Where do they live? What's the problem you're trying to solve for them? What's your idea? Why is your idea better than their current solution?" We asked each fellow to answer these questions honestly. Once we all stated our goals, the entire room made a social contract to each other. We promised to be partners from that moment onward, holding each other accountable every step of the way. On good days, on dark days, and all the days in between.

We made a pact that we — strangers — would become friends.

This was one of those pivotal moments when we all realized the power of what we were doing. If we were successful in this project, in six months, we'd see 25 new businesses run by 25 friends who would also emerge as leaders in their communities. Nigeria would be a better place because we did this together.

Later in the week, there was excitement in the air as we participated in a hackathon to build prototypes. Despite the rolling blackouts and overworked wi-fi, it was all-hands on deck to get the prototypes ready for Friday afternoon.

The final presentation of each of the prototypes at the end of the day on Friday was an emotional one. Each of the fellows showcased what they'd created that week… and what they were going to do next. It was incredible to see one-line ideas turn into realistic business plans in such a short space of time. This really drove home for all of us the importance of creating a very rough prototype simply to test the concept. By putting a timeframe to it, no one had time to stress about how long or how many resources it would take. Every single fellow had something to demo by the end of the week.

We were humbled by the passion and creativity these entrepreneurs showed in trying to create better economic opportunities for themselves and their loved ones, while making their country an even better place for everyone. We learned so much from their endless optimism and positivity even as they tackled some of the hardest business model and technical challenges.

Originally we'd fallen in love with 25 ideas on paper. That week we fell in love with the 25 people making those ideas come to life.

By the end of the week, the fellows and our team had become the closest of friends. Our many communication channels (WhatsApp and our not-very-secret Facebook group) have been buzzing with activity at all hours of the day and night for years now. If you ask anyone in our crew, we'll unanimously tell you that the fellowship has been one of the most energizing and rewarding things we've done in our lives.

We were so moved by the life-changing work of our Nigerian fellows and amazed at how much we were learning that we realized we needed to do another fellowship. This time, we chose East Africa to meet a different group of entrepreneurs and understand the local issues they were taking on.

On the flight from Lagos to Nairobi, we started writing down what had worked and what had not with our first fellowship, and an outline of what the week should look like. Little did we know that we were writing the Sh#tty First Draft of this book (more on this super-sophisticated tactic later).

Since then, we've refined that outline 46 times, once for every business we've worked with. This book itself is the 47th iteration of the framework — Model 47. We wrote this down formally for two reasons:

1. To share the method. This method has worked on 46 entrepreneurs in both emerging and developed markets, whether the entrepreneur has a formal education or a broad network such as many of the entrepreneurs in Silicon Valley tend to have. We believe some or all of these techniques will work for you as well.
2. To share the stories. Entrepreneurship can sometimes be a lonely, scary journey. You are not alone. If you ever feel like you are, come talk to us and our fellows. We're real people and we are VERY excited to meet you.

Find us at: http://Facebook.com/groups/model47

Whether you live in London or Liberia, San Francisco or Sao Paolo, Portland or Port Harcourt, this book is for you. We believe in you. We hope you find this book useful as you build your business.

Over and over, we've seen people help their families and their communities by starting businesses to address real, consumer needs. Entrepreneurs create jobs, put food on the table, and inspire hope. You are one of them. There is some sort of change you want to see in the world. It may only be a faint outline right now; maybe the sculpture hasn't fully emerged from the stone. Unfortunately, there are likely an incredible, staggering amount of HARD days in front of you. But you are not alone, by any means. Once we started writing Model 47, we realized there was so much more we wanted to learn and share with non-traditional creators like our fellow. We decided to start our own business called Origin Stories, providing non-traditional creators (such as yourself) the DIY (do-it-yourself) kit to be a badass in business including the business of YOU. Dona's Prima Dona fashion business is the "coat or armor" for those in the Origin Stories community. Jeremiah's consulting business

Boxes and Foxes helps solve specific problems in a 1:1 format for those in the Origin Stories community.

We've heard over and over that real-life examples of people who are currently on the entrepreneurship journey are incredibly helpful. People who are having wins and losses every day. We've provided examples from at least one of our 46 entrepreneurs in each chapter; a different one for each so you get to understand a lot of diverse kinds of businesses. For continuity, we've also provided examples from our own businesses: Origin Stories, Prima Dona and Boxes and Foxes. We're all in this together.

We wrote this book in cars, on airport floors and in airplanes. For months, wherever we've been, we've set the timer for 20 minutes. We do work sprints: we create as fast as we can without overthinking. The first draft always sucks. It's terrible! But we don't give up. We iterate. We edit and refine it. We show it to our friends, they laugh at us, then we refine some more — it gets better. Slowly. This technique has led to magical results and extreme clarity. We highly recommend you do this with each section: open the book, look at the time on your phone, your watch or the clock on the wall, and… Go! Work for 20 minutes. Stop, and assess. If you have more time, do another sprint.

Throughout this journey, you'll find yourself arriving at "*eureka*" moments. But also "*what am I going to do?!*" moments and "*who the heck am I going to call*" moments. We highly recommend that instead of trying to solve everything at that moment, you write the points down and tackle them with a clear mind. We've created a "Progress Tracking" section at the end of the book where you can track these things.

There's also The Model 47 Workbook which accompanies this book and has the questions we ask and space for your own answers. We created and used the workbook extensively while creating our Origin Stories business. While we highly recommend you get the workbook to make your life easier, but you can also do all the work in your own blank notebook.

The vision is that by the time you complete all of the chapters across the three major acts of your business, you'll have written down a clear business plan.

If you need help at any point, CONTACT US! We REALLY want to co-create with you. We want more lessons and stories to put into version two of this book as well as on our website. If you find glaring holes in topics that you'd like to see us cover in more detail, let us know. We want to co-create with you (we talk endlessly about that topic in this book). You can find us and the 46 entrepreneurs who inspired this book here: http://Facebook.com/groups/model47

If you're reading this book, you're like us. You're a Taiwo. You're not okay with the status quo. You're ready to make a difference. You might not be 100% ready, but you're going to do the thing anyway.

Our mission is to help 1000 non-traditional entrepreneurs make a profit every year. Are you ready to be one of these profitable ones?

If so, let's get a work sprint on. Set the time for 20 minutes and flip the page.

❧ ACT I ❧

Will You Have Customers for Your Idea?

I t's our goal that, in addition to reading the stories of entrepreneurs just like you, you'll be filling out your notebook. At the end of this, you'll have a full business plan down on paper.

By the end of Act 1, these are the tools you'll have (about one page for each):

- ❧ What is the overview of your idea? (We call this our "Sh#tty First Draft.)
- ❧ Your "Why Me" Statement
- ❧ Who Is Your Hero? (Build for One)
- ❧ Problem Definition
- ❧ Solution Sketch
- ❧ Alternatives (Competition) and Differentiators
- ❧ Segmentation (Finding the Gowons)
- ❧ Target Audience(s)
- ❧ Positioning
- ❧ Value Proposition
- ❧ List of Riskiest Assumptions
- ❧ Riskiest Assumption Test (RAT)
- ❧ Minimum Viable Product (MVP)
- ❧ Co-Create Loop
- ❧ Your near and future goals

Write Down the Sh#tty First Draft

"I want to turn on every single light in Nigeria. Then in Africa."

On the first day of our fellowship bootcamp in Lagos, Nigeria, Yeshua Russell compelled us immediately. It wasn't just that the choir director and entrepreneur *sang* his greeting.

"How aaarreee you, my neeeew friendssss?"

Nor was it ONLY the luminesce of his smile. Seriously, his smile can scare off even the deepest of cynics.

No, the thing that stood out MOST to us was the crystal clarity and stunning expanse of the young man's vision. His dreams were continental.

Throughout the grueling first day of bootcamp, Yeshua never lost his smile or his focus. He wanted to provide electricity to his community, his country, his continent. Curious, we sat next to the GrouPower CEO at dinner to hear his origin story. We wanted to learn more. Why were his aspirations so grand?

Yeshua was born into a middle-class family in the city of Abuja, Nigeria that ran an engineering company. Though Yeshua studied architecture and worked at his family's firm for a while, the entrepreneurship bug chomped on him. He started up a broadband communications network business. Due to his lack of tech background, Yeshua stayed up late nights learning how to run an internet service provider (ISP) so that his community could access the internet.

To keep his business open even when the electricity went out (as it often did in Abuja), Yeshua and his partners installed solar panels and battery banks in his firm's base-stations and offices. One day, Yeshua was negotiating with customers when suddenly a rolling blackout struck. The customers were astonished that Yeshua's office stayed lit even though the rest of the neighborhood went pitch black. They asked Yeshua to set them up with a solar system as well. As more people began to demand this technology, Yeshua and his co-workers began to install solar systems for customers as a side-hustle.

One night years later, Yeshua was working late when the electricity went out again. As he switched over the lights in his office to run from solar-powered batteries, Yeshua looked out the window and realized the medical center next door was bathed in darkness.

This was not good.

The next day Yeshua learned that a patient had died the previous night because the machine keeping her alive had lost power. Yeshua recalls the devastated wails of her family, how broken her husband looked.

Yeshua was deeply disturbed by this incident. For days, he couldn't stop thinking about it. Why did this have to happen? Why didn't the medical center have generators? Or better yet, solar power? Lack of electricity had killed that woman. How many other families would have to suffer?

As Yeshua searched for answers to these questions, he realized there was no one tackling the problem in Abuja. The thought haunted him for three weeks. Four weeks later, on a Monday, Yeshua decided that he needed to be the one to solve it.

He had no idea what he was going to do exactly, or how he was going to do it. Yet, he knew the work needed to be done. No more patients should die when the electricity goes out.

When he heard about our fellowship program, he jumped at the opportunity to really make this business happen. When Yeshua first arrived at bootcamp, his initial concept involved providing solar power to hospitals, clinics, and rural residential clusters. Together we worked through the business plan. In doing so, we realized that potential customers in rural areas would have trouble getting the necessary credit to pay for a solar panel installation. This meant that Yeshua would first need to test out his operations with larger-scale, paying customers before moving into hospitals and clinics, where failure could mean someone's death. To gain credibility and experience, therefore, Yeshua decided to focus initially on business customers.

In the six months that followed, Yeshua solidified his business plan and inked deals with three local businesses. Since then, GrouPower has also provided solar energy to four schools — two of these are government-owned and located in rural areas that previously hadn't had access to electricity at all. The solar systems allow the students to use their center which had gone unutilized for months due to power supply issues. In addition, GrouPower has also installed solar power systems on three farms, two pharmacies and a medical clinic.

Yeshua never forgets his mission to turn on ALL the lights in Nigeria, and not just for businesses. He's just signed a deal with JAIZ Bank to provide solar systems on a lease-to-own basis to qualified customers.

Yeshua recently presented his work at the InterSolar Conference in Munich, where his presentation was rated as Best in Show. He presented the same material he created for our fellowship graduation in 2017.

They're doing it. Yeshua and his team are providing renewable energy to entire communities. We've been incredibly proud and honored to watch GrouPower transform from a fledgling idea to truly living out the mission of turning on the lights in Nigeria. You can find them in Abuja, Nigeria as well as at https://groupower.com.ng.

When Yeshua first arrived at bootcamp, he arrived with what we fondly call a Sh#tty First Draft. Fiction writers use this technique to capture their story on paper no matter how bad it is.

> We believe that first drafts *should* be terrible. They should be a complete brain-dump of what's in your head.

Once you've written down all of your convoluted thoughts, you can start to organize the mess into something that makes more sense — then edit further from there. Yeshua's Sh#tty First Draft was this:

ଔ *Sell solar power panels to hospitals and clinics in Abuja that can't afford to lose power, then moving onto homes*

ଔ *Using the tech he already knew how to build*

ଔ *Charging per solar unit*

ଔ *No one else is doing this in Abuja*

ଔ *This provides good impact to the community and once proven can also be sold to schools and homes so children can get a better education and study, even when the power goes out.*

We wrote the Sh#tty First Draft of this book in a well-worn notebook and one time on napkins when we ran out of pages in a van during a roadtrip from Lagos to Ibadan in Nigeria. It was a pretty bad first draft, but it was a start. We evolved our draft into half-done chapters in OneNote, then into worksheets we printed out for the founders we worked with. Many steps later, we arrived at the words you're reading today.

Prima Dona Example

Dona has been thinking about her fashion line, Prima Dona for about six years, but never took the time to formally make a business plan. She has recently done this using this book. This is her Sh#tty First Draft.

Prima Dona is:

ଔ A line of fashion for people who are AND people—those who need pieces that will work across their busy, multi-faceted lives

ଔ Statement clothing for powerful people — those who have a statement to make

- ☙ Designed in Seattle, made in Kenya and Nigeria by local tailors in those countries
- ☙ Work with Leah on finding tailors and translating specifications for Kenya as a version one test.
- ☙ Made to order, tailor starts work only once an order is place — reduces waste
- ☙ Each print is only available till the fabric bolt runs out
- ☙ Some items will be reversible
- ☙ A showcase of the customers on the website
- ☙ Pricing will be what people feel is right for them based on belonging to a global movement of people who are reducing waste and creating jobs for emerging market tailors.

Boxes and Foxes Example

Jeremiah created Boxes and Foxes consulting after realizing he gets asked the same questions over and over again. *Is my business going to make money? If not, how can I actually make money?*

He realized that, over the years, he's informally helped friends and friends-of-friends gain clarity on their plans and bring profit to their businesses. He decided to formalize his side hustle, and build Boxes and Foxes into a real business of his own. To do this, he went through the 30 steps of this book.

- ☙ *What is your product/service? Bespoke consulting services helping non-traditional entrepreneurs solve some of the challenges they're facing. The two elements are:*
    - ☙ A series of specific materials that are tailored to the business (worksheets, etc).
    - ☙ Hour-long conversation with an entrepreneur to tackle one of their challenges.
- ☙ *Who are the customers and why do they need your solution?*
    - ☙ Non-traditional founders who never went to business school and really don't know many people who have MBAs or have started businesses. These founders are scrappy and experimental self-starters. They just need info on a few specific things.

    ভ *What makes it different?*

        ◆ It doesn't assume a fancy degree or a large network. Assumes a desire to work hard and be scrappy. Helps both tried-and-true businesses that exist (coffee shop, bookstore, etc), but also unique businesses that answer questions such as how can you use the pay as you wish model; how do you encourage gender studies in product development; how do you save the lives of rural, poor pregnant women who can't afford healthcare?

    ভ *How could you create it and what will you need to do so?*

        ◆ I'm going to set up a website with a description of the service. Make printable worksheets. Schedule time with founders.

    ভ *How will it make money?*

        ◆ Charge a small fee for tailored worksheets

        ◆ Charge an hourly fee for customized consulting time.

    ভ *What is your long-term vision for what it could be?*

        ◆ I'll see many of the founders I've helped become successful.

    ভ *What other uses or positive impacts could it have on the community in the long-term?*

        ◆ Many founders I've guided have helped their communities. They're saving lives and making the world an equal place. I'm also saving founder's precious time so they can focus on growing their business.

You're reading this book because you have some sort of an idea for a business. What is that idea?

Today, just like we all did, you're going to write down a Sh#tty First Draft of your business idea. It's not going to be — and in fact it SHOULDN'T be — fully-fleshed out yet. No detailed business plan at this point. That's what the rest of the book is for. Today, you just need to write down the vague business idea in your workbook or journal. Bullet-point form is just fine!

Now go to your notebook and let's get to work. What's your business idea's Sh#tty First Draft?

Your Sh#tty First Draft should:

- Be short (typically 2 - 6 bulleted lines)
- May include some or all of these:
    - What is your product/service?
    - Who are the customers and why do they need it?
    - What makes it different?
    - How could you create it and what will you need to do so?
    - How will it make money?
    - What is your long-term vision for what it could be?
    - What other uses or positive impacts could it have on the community in the long-term?
    (keeping in mind that all of this will change many times as you define it)

Put it away for a few days, think more, then rewrite and build on the ideas. Don't be afraid to be wrong or have an incomplete draft if you don't have all the answers yet.

Declare Why You

When we met Dr. Moses Keller, his business was a dream written on sheets of paper. His origin story deeply saddened us. As he told it, more and more of our crew quietly gathered around him to listen. His story affirmed not only the need for the Nigeria fellowship, but also the East Africa fellowship six months later. Truth be told, his story resulted in this book. Most work doesn't save actual lives. Dr. Moses's work definitely does.

When he was a young obstetrician-gynecologist (ob-gyn), just graduated from medical school, Dr. Moses worked as a resident in a clinic in Port Harcourt, Nigeria. He specialized in delivering babies.

On this night, a woman from a more rural part of Port Harcourt was brought into the clinic. She was nine months pregnant... and bleeding heavily. Dr. Moses and the birth attendants discovered that the woman's placenta was blocking her birth passage.

No one knew this because the woman had never had an ultrasound before. Despite trying their best to save her life, Dr. Moses and his attendants were too late. Mrs. Hope Ofori died on the delivery bed, and her unborn child along with her.

Crushingly, Hope Ofori's story is not uncommon. According to UNICEF, one in 13 pregnant Nigerian women die in pregnancy or childbirth. 58,000 Nigerian women die every year, and 159 women die each DAY, from preventable complications in pregnancy and childbirth.

Haunted by the memory of Hope Ofori and horrified to learn how common these deaths were, Dr. Moses realized he had to do more. He started a social business called SonoCare. His initial vision for SonoCare was to drive his Honda Saloon around Nigeria providing mobile ultrasounds to the women who need it most —those such as Hope, who live in the most rural parts of Nigeria where ultrasounds are rare and expensive.

That evening, after the entire crew had gone for dinner, the two of us sat with Dr. Moses. There was a power outage (seriously, half our stories involve power outages), but our laptops were charged so we used their screens for light. For the next three hours, Dr. Moses listed his goals, his costs, and his challenges. It became so obvious to us (and a few eavesdroppers) that if someone was going to be able to solve this problem, it was going to be him.

That night, over spicy *jollof* rice and chicken *suya*, we sorted through his business and tech needs and came up with a plan.

Since that night in Lagos, he has executed on this plan; all day, every day, surpassing even his own high expectations.

The first thing Dr. Moses did was lead a crowdfund on Indiegogo for USD $16,000 to purchase the equipment he needed for SonoCare. With the funds he raised, he bought a mobile ultrasound machine as well as an ECG machine. Armed with these new devices and a laptop to run his business, he spent two days in Diobu Waterfront — a low-income, rural community in southern Nigeria with no healthcare facilities. He performed screenings for 116 women who had never had ultrasounds before. His tests found that 72 of the women (62% of the women screened) had high-risk pregnancies. Of all the women he examined, 22 of them *didn't even know they were pregnant*. Remarkable results in just two days. These women have now been able to provide this information to their birth attendants, which dramatically increases their chance of survival, Today, Dr. Moses continues to pursue grants, donations and other funding options to keep costs low for the rural women unable to afford the $8 price per sonogram. You can find more information at http://www.sonocare.com.ng/

This entrepreneurial life can be hard. There are going to be days, months, YEARS when you might not make money.

To persevere, you have to TRULY believe that you are
The One who's going to solve this problem. Otherwise,
you will always be exploring your other options.

As we coached our entrepreneurs using Model 47, at this point we asked everyone these three questions:

1. Why are YOU the one to tackle this problem?
2. What qualifications DO you have that make you more qualified than others (specialized knowledge, access to customers, a unique idea or technology, a strong ability to execute on the idea, etc)?
3. What qualifications DON'T you have, and how can you get these (education/ experience, hiring people who have them, partner with other organizations that do, etc)?

We're both painfully aware that starting a business is not easy. It's vital to identify early on which parts of your business will present the most challenges so that you can look out for opportunities to learn the required skills or find people to help you.

For Dr. Moses

Why are you the one to tackle the problem?
He's an expert in the field. When he speaks on this topic, people listen. He's tested thousands of patients. He has written books on the topic. Moreover, he's clearly committed to combat Nigerian maternal mortality. He could have gotten a comfortable doctor's job tending to wealthy families in Lagos, Nigeria and left this problem for someone else to solve. Yet he refuses to do that because of the experiences he's had. Nigerian maternal mortality is a problem that he is not only ABLE to solve, but desperately WANTS to solve and is COMMITTED to solving;

no matter how much effort or cost goes into it. Why Dr. Moses? *Because he must.* It's obvious to everyone he talks to.

What qualifications DO you have?
He's a medical doctor with a decade of experience in diagnostic imaging and reproductive health.

What qualifications DON'T you have?
While Dr. Moses is highly qualified to tackle aspects of Nigerian maternal mortality, there was a good deal he was NOT qualified to do. He didn't know much about the financial aspect of running a business. He's a doctor, not an entrepreneur. He didn't go to business school. A year ago, he didn't know what a "break-even" was (to be honest, neither did Dona), or why he needed one. But he had a vision, an amazing one; one that can save the lives of countless women and their infants. The parts where he needed help, he talked with us and our crew. Dr. Moses built a team around himself, people with these complementary skills, including his advisory board. He was able to build this business successfully because he is the one who MUST do this work.

Prima Dona Example

Why are YOU the one to tackle this problem?

- ᐇ Dona is an AND person—someone who has to go from an office job to speaking on stage to an evening social event with no time to change clothes. She knows exactly what kind of wardrobe she needs for this.
- ᐇ Her grandmother ran her own tailoring business where she created hand-crafted clothing for women for the most important days of their lives. She built a long-lasting community of people around her doing this.

- ❧ Dona speaks in public often and loves clothing that's stand-out and statement, not just plain and forgettable. She fell in love with the fabrics she saw in Nigeria and Kenya.
- ❧ Dona want to create jobs for people in emerging markets.

What qualifications DO you have?

- ❧ Dona attended fashion design school and has a natural ability to predict what will look good without having to "see" it first.
- ❧ Dona has a connection with Leah Otieno who is a clothing matchmaker — she matches people with tailors in Kenya.
- ❧ Dona a big network of people who will be interested in this service and will be happy to test her products.

What qualifications DON'T you have?

- ❧ Dona's never made or sold a "hardware" product before — as in a physical product — only software.
- ❧ Dona's never done business where a key partner is overseas in Kenya.
- ❧ Dona's never had to work with something as emotional and subjective as fashion. Software and books (her other businesses) aren't emotional.
- ❧ Dona has no experience with the financial aspect of running a business. What the heck is a break-even, anyway?
- ❧ Dona mitigate most of these by treating this business as a learning experiment; testing on a small group of very patient customers, seeking mentorship from a friend who has created (and shut down) a fashion line.

Boxes and Foxes Example

Why are YOU the one to tackle this problem?

- ଔ Jeremiah has the skills and experience to do this. He's done this in 20 countries and in 3 languages for people across nearly every industry.
- ଔ More importantly, he WANTS to do this — he believes one of the best ways to empower local communities is to create job and this directly helps to create jobs.
- ଔ Jeremiah gets inspired by meeting other founders and love hearing about what they're doing and love helping them solve their challenges.

What qualifications DO you have?

- ଔ Jeremiah has a MBA from Wharton.
- ଔ He has worked at Strategy Consulting at BCG, Deloitte, and AMS.
- ଔ He has done this in 20 countries and in 3 languages for people across nearly every industry.
- ଔ He's worked for and with over a hundred startups all over the world.

What qualifications DON'T you have, and how can you get these?

- ଔ Time. Jeremiah is not able to commit to doing this full-time.
- ଔ He's not an expert in every industry.
- ଔ He's never charged for this work before.
- ଔ He's never advertised this skillset to strangers before.

Now it's your turn

Go ahead and answer the next set of questions in your workbook VERY HONESTLY. Unless you show it to someone, no one will see this but you. Be honest and vulnerable with yourself. This will become very important later.

Why is this problem important to YOU? Why are YOU the one who MUST solve this problem?

Why are YOU qualified to solve this problem? What qualifications / skills / experiences / knowledge do you bring to the table? (specialized knowledge, access to customers, a unique idea or technology, a strong ability to execute on the idea, etc)?

And of course, the inverse: what do you NOT know? What will you need to learn or need help with?(education/experience, hiring people who have them, partner with other organizations that do, etc)?

Build for One

There's no better way to describe Olayinka (Yinka) Olanrewaju than "presidential." Articulate and confident, Yinka sees the best in everyone; the value in every situation. Yinka quickly emerged as a leader in our bootcamp. From day one, other fellows turned to him for help and advice. It was no surprise to us when Yinka told us his dream was LITERALLY to become President of Nigeria. From an early age, he was determined to spend his life improving the lives of others in an ethical and honorable way. He saw no better way to do this than being the leader of his country. However, the sudden death of his father disrupted these plans — Yinka went to law school and sought a stable job at a law firm to support his mother.

Still, in the back of his mind remained his personal mission: to leave every situation better than he had found it. He found his opportunity at the Abuja campus of the Nigerian Law School, while earning an extra credit he needed. He struck up a friendship with a talented yet petrified young law student named Tade. Yinka discovered a startling fact: nearly 50% of the law students in Nigeria failed. Unable to pass exam after exam, students helplessly watched their dreams evaporate. Yinka realized that Tade and many of his peers struggled with the methods of teaching common in Nigeria at the time: One lecturer. 200 students. Lots of theory. Few practical activities. Little class engagement.

Yinka nabbed Tade as a mentee. He coached him extensively in a more practical, more hands-on way with real-life situations Yinka himself had encountered in his law practice. It worked. Tade passed his tests and the bar exam. He was off!

A daring idea emerged for Yinka. To test his theory, he created a focus group of 20 other law students like Tade, hoping to improve even further his content and methods. After coaching this group and watching them also succeed, Yinka realized that he could create more value *teaching* law than practicing the law himself. Glowing feedback from previously-struggling students who now passed their tests confirmed his purpose in life.

Yinka hadn't felt this excited since dreaming of becoming President of Nigeria. He realized there was a clear need, and he was the one who could solve this problem. By tackling this challenge, he could help even more people achieve their dreams. Yinka thought the opportunity to disrupt the largely static and stale legal education was both irresistible and worthy.

He assembled a talented team of colleagues to build Lawcademy, an e-learning platform using interactive content to explain complex legal subjects in easy-to-understand terms. Using the same content he'd shared with Tade and friends, Yinka created digital learning tools such as videos, mind-mapping, infographics, and quizzes that gave students instant feedback on their performance WHILE using practical examples from the West African market.

Yinka built Lawcademy for Tade — ONE real live person who was also unbiased. Tade was NOT a close friend of Yinka before this whole experiment began, so he could be unbiased as to the usefulness of Lawcademy and give real feedback as opposed not wanting to hurt Yinka's feelings or risk the relationship.

This is why Tade is the hero of the Lawcademy story. By focusing on his hero, Yinka could assess the problem he was seeking to solve. He could learn how much this real person would pay for the service. Rather than building for a customer segment or a made-up persona, he could test his idea in real time with Tade before spending time and money on an expensive solution.

Building for one is a concept that was drilled into our entrepreneurs (and us!) by Femi Longe, one of the co-founders of Co-Creation Hub. During the entire first day of our fellowship program, Femi challenged each fellow with detailed questions about their hero: "who is your customer? No really, what's their name? What's their phone number?" Everyone squirmed and tried to escape this questioning.

Ultimately, the most successful of our fellows have been those who were able to name a specific real live person who was the hero of their story.

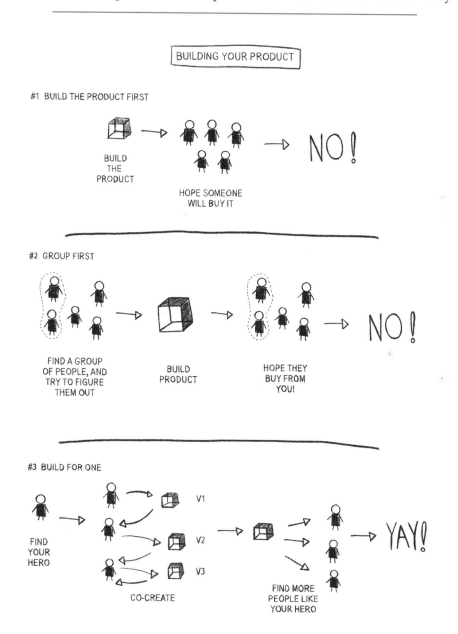

BUILDING YOUR PRODUCT

#1 BUILD THE PRODUCT FIRST

BUILD THE PRODUCT

HOPE SOMEONE WILL BUY IT

NO!

#2 GROUP FIRST

FIND A GROUP OF PEOPLE, AND TRY TO FIGURE THEM OUT

BUILD PRODUCT

HOPE THEY BUY FROM YOU!

NO!

#3 BUILD FOR ONE

FIND YOUR HERO

V1
V2
V3

CO-CREATE

FIND MORE PEOPLE LIKE YOUR HERO

YAY!

Prima Dona Example

The one person Dona is building her business for and with is:

- ☞ *Hero's Name?*
  Ioana Tanase
- ☞ *Where do they live?*
  London, United Kingdom
- ☞ *Their profession?*
  Recruiter for Microsoft by day and the founder of a small side-business called Track and Fuel by night. She is also an artist by weekend.
- ☞ *How to contact?*
  WhatsApp
- ☞ *Do you have contact info?*
  Yes
- ☞ *Their spending power?*
  Medium
- ☞ *Why have you selected them?*
  - ❧ Ioana loves fashion that no one else has and that has a story attached to it
  - ❧ She loves to give back
  - ❧ She has an "AND" life — she is truly multi-faceted creator who has a clear statement to make… and needs a wardrobe to match
- ☞ *What problem are you solving for them and how important is it to them (high/medium/low)?*
  She needs help finding fashion that works for all the aspects of her life, is one-of-a kind, has a great story AND creates jobs and visibility for tailors in emerging markets. This is of Medium importance to Ioana
- ☞ *What benefit would your solution have in their life?*
  This will benefit Ioana by helping her stand-out in her job, speaking engagements and side-hustles AND fulfill her desire to give back.

Boxes and Foxes Example

The one single person Jeremiah is building for is:

- *Hero's Name?*
  Rachel Elsinga
- *Where do they live?*
  Amsterdam, the Netherlands
- *Their profession?*
  Banker and now founder of a startup that helps NGOs and companies create products that are more inclusive specifically to women.
- *How to contact?*
  WhatsApp
- *Do you have contact info?*
  Yes
- *Their spending power?*
  High
- *Why have you selected them?*
  Unique business model that has never been done before i.e. how to charge and who to charge. Jeremiah believes in this work.
- *What problem are you solving for them and how important is it to them (high/ medium/low)?*
  She needs help building a business around promoting gender equality in product design. High importance to them.
- *What benefit would your solution have in their life?*
  She would be able to empower women all over the world.

For you to guarantee your idea will work, it will need to be specific enough to help a real human being. Pick ONE SINGLE PERSON. Of course, you'll want to help an entire group of people (such as farmers, commuters, or mothers), but for now let's focus on one single person, who may or may not represent the needs of a larger group. Describe them as best you can. Do you know them personally? What's their spending power? Is this someone you can pick up the phone and call or text? If not, you should probably get to know him or her better. Once you truly understand this person and their needs, you can reach out to others like them because you know you can provide a clear value to them, just as Yinka did.

Sometimes the single human you are building for won't be an end-user customer, but rather be representing an organization like a business, a school or a hospital. By helping these organizations tackle a problem more efficiently, you will be ensuring that they create more value for their own end users or customers. This was the case for Omasirichukwu Udeinya, who accidentally discovered his business while studying Computer Science at the American University of Nigeria. Omasiri's database class professor gave the class an assignment where they had to identify a problem in their local community and solve it.

Since Omasiri's parents both worked in the medical field, he went with his comfort zone — the school clinic. At the university clinic, he met Antonia Njike Fonkam, the forward-thinking clinic administrator. Before writing hundreds of lines of code, Omasiri listened carefully to Antonia, seeking to understand her needs. Antonia was excited because they had already started to use Microsoft Excel to store patient information. Digital patient records would be way better. She pointed Omasiri to a cabinet of patient heath files — all written on paper, and described how difficult it was to keep track of and find patient information quickly.

Omasiri imagined what would happen if his sister went to the clinic for an emergency and they couldn't find her records. With no information, her doctor would need to make potentially life-threatening decisions based on guesswork.

He realized this was the case for millions of Nigerians. He had to do something about this.

Omasiri came up with an idea to make Antonia's life easier, and the clinic safer. He built her a simple web app that contained just two things: a form for registering new patients and another form for recording their visits. He stored this information in a simple database. He then deployed this to Antonia.

Antonia used the web app to register new patients. As she had questions or ran into bugs, she gave real-time feedback to Omasiri for necessary changes. Soon everyone at the clinic was using the web app and Omasiri implemented more features for them. Once Omasiri realized Antonia and her clinic found his solution useful, he knew he had on his hands a business that would work. Chart Synergy was born.

Today, Chart Synergy helps healthcare providers gather, manage and understand their patient data better. With this tech, hospitals and clinics can run more efficiently and safely by reducing long wait times for patients, freeing up the space in cabinets taken up by paper files, and improving care since doctors can access accurate and comprehensive patient records. You can sign up for a demo at: http://www.chartsynergy.com/

Omasiri didn't randomly wander around to hospitals and clinics, trying to build a tool for all of them. He chose ONE person in ONE business who is unbiased and has a real problem… and he solved it for her. By doing that, he built a tool that could be adapted to reach many people with similar needs; and by working with them in the future, he could add new features to make it more valuable and scalable to others. When multiple options are available to solve a problem, honing your solution to a super-niche audience can be an excellent way to start. You can always expand your audience later after mastering the first customer group.

So breaking it down, you need to know some basic things about the person you're trying to help.

Hero's name	Tade	Antonia
Where do they live?	Abuja, Nigeria	Yola, Nigeria
Their profession?	Law student	Medical Clinic Administrator
How to contact?	Smartphone/in-person	In-person
Do you have contact info?	Yes!	Yes!
Their spending power?	Medium	Medium
Why have you selected them as your hero?	Very talented and hard-working, he just needs some extra coaching.	She's up for trying new technology to make life better for hospital employees and patients
What problem do they need help with and how important is it in their life (high/medium/low)	He needs help understanding law school concepts. It's extremely important for his career and future - high	She needs help making her job easier and less manual. It's very important to her career and future - high.
What benefit would your solution have in their life?	He would understand legal concepts, pass their exams and become a lawyer.	She'd be able to take on more challenges in her job rather than tracking paper records. She'd grow in her career. She'd also be seen as a technical leader by working with Omasiri.

So now it's your turn

Who is the hero of your story? You will build for them and then scale to many like them.

We highly recommend you do NOT choose a close friend or family member who will automatically use your product/service and not give you feedback like a normal customer.

Fill out the table in your workbook with your own hero's information.

- ଓ Hero's Name?
- ଓ Where do they live?
- ଓ Their profession?
- ଓ How to contact?
- ଓ Do you have contact info?
- ଓ Their spending power?
- ଓ Why have you selected them?
- ଓ What do they need help with and how important is it to them (high/medium/low)?
- ଓ What benefit would your solution have in their life?

Understand the Real Problem

We were profoundly moved by the life-changing work of our Nigerian fellows. We learned a great deal from them and realized we needed to do another fellowship to keep learning. We chose Kenya as home base for our East Africa fellowship and welcomed entrepreneurs from Kenya, Uganda, Rwanda and Tanzania into the cohort.

On the first day of the East Africa fellowship, we met Alfred Onegere — a Telecommunications and Information Engineering student who was taking on a very challenging situation with global implications: refugee safety and security.

We sat down with this ambitious young man to understand why he chose this problem instead of getting a "normal day job" with his tech skills. He explained to us that his eyes had been opened to the plight of refuges. After meeting them and hearing their stories, he could no longer go back to his ordinary world of a 9am to 5pm day job, going home and watching TV and hanging with friends.

Alfred told us the heartbreaking origin story that motivated him to help refugees.

Desperate to flee Syria, a young man named Hassan and his best friend Tarek sold their life's possessions to buy seats on a rubber dinghy bound for Greece. Neither knew how to swim, so they bought the only life jackets they could afford.

Four miles off the coast of Syria, a squall hit their battered dinghy. Their boat was overloaded; full of desperate families and their belongings. Lashed by the rain and waves, the boat filled with water and started to sink. To lighten the load, the refugees threw overboard all their life's possessions, but too late. Dark heavy waves swamped the dinghy, and 23 men, women and children went into the frigid water.

Hassan's life jacket did the expected — it kept him afloat. Hassan saw his friend Tarek splashing in the water, several feet away. To his horror, he realized that Tarek's lifejacket was disintegrating. It was fake. Hassan tried to reach his only friend in the world, but it was too late. Tarek slid into the Aegean Sea, and Hassan never saw him again.

After Alfred heard Hassan's story, he lay awake all night. By morning, he'd vowed to help the many refugees in his home country of Kenya.

Over many months, Alfred visited three different camps in Kenya — Ruiru, Komarock and Kaberia. As he spent time talking with refugees he met there, he sought to understand the problems they faced.

The refugees told Alfred stories of unpredictable weather. When it rained hard near the Kalobeyei Settlement, water tore through the camp. Parents screamed helplessly as the raging water swept away their children, drowning them. Only moments earlier, children had been out playing happily in the drizzle. No one had known the waters were rising rapidly.

They told him stories of rampant disease. A cholera outbreak killed seven Sudanese refugees In Kalobeyei camp. The camp's latrines were full and people had dug new pits. No one realized they needed a permit for new latrines to ensure ample distance from drinking water.

They told him stories of corruption. Refugees couldn't access medical services without an identification card, but could get that card if they bribed officials $200 — money which most refugees did not have.

After spending weeks talking with his new friends, Alfred realized that many of the refugees' challenges (while super complex and multi-dimensional) could be to some extent linked to a single issue — their lack of trustworthy information. Because many refugees had been uprooted from their homes, families, friends, and support networks, they faced a tremendous disadvantage. They didn't even know what they did or didn't know; what they needed to know for their survival. They didn't know who the honest merchants were; where to find the safe places to sleep for the night; where to find potential jobs.

Alfred wondered if he could provide these refugees with trustworthy information based on data and reputation. He could help them construct a support network of valuable opportunities validated by people's reputations. His vision was to create a version of existing member networks such as Uber and AirBnB, where people trust strangers to drive them home or lodge them. Why not something similar for refugees?

By digging down deep and taking the time to understand the problems facing this community, Alfred was able to identify a real way to help them. He founded Sahibu — a member network for refugees offering information and opportunities, built on reputation and trust. Because he knew *exactly* for whom he was building a service, he built Sahibu to work on feature phones, the devices refugees tend to have.

One thing that's surprised Alfred (and us) was that refugees not only used Sahibu to exchange vital information and advice, but also to spread music and art among the community. The most recent articles on Sahibu are about refugee-created and run art shows and concerts in the camps.

Alfred used his personal funds to start this business, and soon ran out of money. Since then, he's had to get a day job to fund his dream. He's come to realize that refugee camps can be quite complex for a business like Sahibu to penetrate and scale properly. The focus group of refugees with whom Alfred co-created Sahibu has really appreciated the work Sahibu is attempting and many of them have started to run more aspects of his business. You can find them at http://Sahibu.info.

Over and over, we've seen founders use this process to seek the results they need.

Before our founders invest time, energy, money, and other precious resources into building a solution, first they identify the root problem their hero faces, and then make sure the hero agrees it is indeed a problem.

Prima Dona Example

For Prima Dona, the exact problem Dona is trying to solve for Ioana Tanase is clothing for all of the aspects of her life that has the "oh my, where did you get that" factor WHILE being ethically made with a good story rather than "I got it at the mall".

Ioana agrees this is the problem she wants solved. Currently, all clothing Ioana finds is mass-produced and everyone in London is wearing it, or *extremely* expensive for something unique that works for her job, travel and side-hustles.

Boxes and Foxes Example

Jeremiah's helping Rachel figure out what to build first and then what they should charge for.

Rachel empathically tells Jeremiah that the business model for their idea is by far the most challenging to figure out, especially since the people paying for their work are often not the end customers.

Now it's your turn

What is the EXACT problem you're trying to solve for the hero you listed above? Have you asked your hero whether this is in fact a big problem in their life?

There are often multiple problems you could seek to solve for a specific person. The specific problem you're going to tackle in many ways drives the exact solution you'll build.

Sketch Your (Initial) Solution

The second person we met during our East Africa fellowship blew our minds with her resilience and hard-working nature. Growing up with little and surviving cancer didn't stop her from starting a business to create jobs in her country.

Leah Otieno was born and raised in a rural town in Kenya called Kokoth-Kateng. She's one of five children born to parents who are *both* teachers and farmers. Her parents instilled in her a deep appreciation for education. During high school, she had the opportunity to live with her aunt in the city of Nairobi, taking full advantage of the higher quality of education. Through diligent study, she completed high school with top scores in the Kenyan National exams. Because of this, she won a full scholarship to Simpson College in the United States. While she majored in Economics with minors in Math and Accounting, she also fell in love with fashion. Her colorful style was quite stand-out in rural Iowa. She used to buy items at thrift stores and create outfits to showcase on a fashion blog. She started learning about fabric and craftsmanship, and honed a deep understanding on how to make a garment long-lasting.

Leah's life was far from easy, however. A long way from home and her family, Leah was diagnosed with Acute Myeloid Leukemia at the beginning of her senior year of college. She was able to get treatment and will officially be in remission in August 2019.

When she returned home to Kenya, Leah found tremendous potential to showcase to the world her country's deep history of textiles and quality tailoring. She came up with the idea of Mshonaji — a way to connect Kenyan fashion with the rest of the world.

Leah realized that local tailoring is a source of income for about 75,000 tailors in Kenya. However, many of the tailors — especially independents who do custom work —lack an effective means to market their services to new clients. Leah also noticed that people overseas had no idea how to get clothing made from unique Kenyan fabrics by reliable tailors.

The vision of Mshonaji is a messaging- and internet-based platform connecting tailors with exceptional skills to an expanded base of customers through reviews, an e-commerce portal, and sophisticated profile and search functions. Mshonaji will offer talented tailors a digital workspace, showcasing their past creations and marketing their specialties. Leah and her team would themselves take pictures of the tailors work and communicate the customer feedback back to the tailors. This is different to Etsy because these highly-skilled tailors often don't have the digital literacy to run an online store AND Mshonaji is created specifically to provide opportunities for local tailors.

Before Leah invested in tech to build Mshonaji's complex review-based website, she wanted to test her idea in the most basic way possible. She sketched out the core parts of her business. Who were the people involved? (The customer needed clothing, the tailors created clothing, and she could connect the two.) What were the transactions between these people? What existing tools could she use to test these transactions?

Initially, she didn't have a website or web portal. Leah decided to interact with clients through SMS texts and messaging apps such as WhatsApp and Facebook Messenger. She spoke with potential clients herself, going back and forth with them to understand exactly what types of garments they were looking for, what their sizes and other preferences were, and what kinds of fabric and colors they wanted. Leah then went to hand-select the fabrics herself, then on to tailors' workshops. She worked closely with tailors to make sure they understood her clients' exact needs through the pictures and detailed instructions. Because Leah spoke both the language of fashion design and was a fashion enthusiast, she was able to translate what the customer wanted to technical specifications for the tailor... since tailors and customers often didn't speak the same language, as in "adjustable" as opposed to "add five inches of seam allowance".

Being the "middle-person" or translator between two very different groups of people who need each other's services is often a profitable and necessary business.

If the client couldn't come in person for a finished garment, Leah delivered it to them — either by courier (for local clients) or through a delivery service (for clients living outside of Nairobi). For example, for Dona she created and delivered to Seattle, Washington a dress made-to-measure from unique fabric found only in one shop in Nairobi.

By running all of these experiments, Leah discovered people are MUCH more likely to order garments if they first see them in person. People want to see, feel and gauge the quality of a finished garment before ordering their own. However, she didn't want to take the risk of setting up a real storefront which would be extremely expensive. She decided to try something interesting. With several of her friends, she'd started a side-business called Lava Latte, a cozy Nairobi-based coffee shop that had comfortable seating for long meetings, hosted live music events and served delicious home-made, fresh food. Leah decided to set up a station for some of her Mshonaji pieces so that people could browse them while they were in the coffee shop. This was an easy way to get her pieces in front of real people without having to set up a formal storefront.

By sketching out the people involved in her business and the different transactions between then using basic boxes and arrows, Leah was able to test a potential solution to her clients' problem without building out an expensive technical solution.

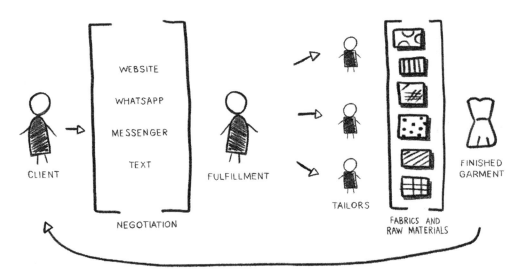

We are all proud customers of Mshonaji's services. We could not be more excited to watch Leah build up her business in a repeatable, scalable and profitable way. Leah's vision of bringing the splendor of Kenyan fashion to the world is well on its way.

<hr />

When we first launched the Nigeria fellowship, we did a scouting trip in Lagos to announce the fellowship to various audiences. A Nigerian radio host named Africanfarmer invited us to come speak on his show aimed at, unsurprisingly, farmers. Africanfarmer taught us some startling facts about Nigerian agriculture.

Agriculture is the largest sector in Nigeria. It contributes 22% of the GDP and employs nearly a third of the country's workforce. However, the lack of innovation in farming and agriculture leads to very high food prices for end customers. For poor urban Nigerians, food takes up nearly 75% of their income! This leads to less money for the education of children and, as such, the cycle of poverty continues.

Because of agriculture's importance to Nigerian growth, we were incredibly excited to welcome soft-spoken farmer and agripreneur Ibrahim Mohammed Aboki as part of the cohort. Ibrahim was born and raised in a community of small-holder farmers, and is extremely proud of his roots as a farmer. After receiving his diploma in renewable energy and interning at a solar company in the urban center of Kano, Nigeria, he started thinking about how renewable energy could help farmers with the challenges they face. These farmers grow tomatoes, corn and other crops; but they would often need to withstand long periods of drought. To irrigate their crops, the farmers would use water pumps powered by petrol (gasoline). However, the high cost of buying petrol often resulted in a significant reduction in farmers' earnings.

To solve this problem, Ibrahim worked with a Mechanical Engineering colleague and they came up with the idea of a solar-powered water pump. They wanted the pump to use as few solar panels as possible and not overheat during operation.

Ibrahim sketched out the business he wanted to build. Each day his workers would fill a wheelbarrow with the gear needed — a water pump for farmers who didn't own one (though several did) and hoses to get the water to the crops. To power one pump, Ibrahim calculated he needed two solar panels. The panels transformed energy from the sun into electricity, running through a charge controller to recharge a battery. Since electricity was stored in the battery as DC (direct current), he then inverted the electricity from DC into AC (alternating current) using an inverter, in order to power the pump. Ibrahim didn't capture every single aspect of Basmalah Enterprises in his quick sketch (for example, he needed salespeople and advertisements to promote his services to new farmers, someplace to store all the gear securely overnight, and someone to schedule daily work), but he was able to jot down the high-level details in his sketch.

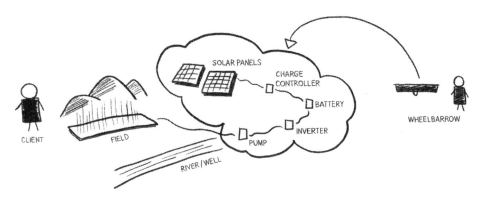

Based on this sketch, Ibrahim and his colleague built the product locally. Today, Basmalah Enterprise's solar irrigation service serves around 500 small-holder farmers and saves them 35% on their crop watering costs while also reducing pollution. One side-effect Ibrahim didn't expect was to create jobs in rural areas. There used to be many unemployed young people who fell into socially violent activities. Basmalah made farming more profitable and attractive to these young people, and in doing so improved their livelihoods as well as that of the community.

Before building their product, all of our entrepreneurs did a basic sketch of this business idea. Who were the people involved? What were the transactions between these people? What existing tools could they use to test these transactions?

Prima Dona Example

The vision of Prima Dona is an ethically made fashion line and community for people who are powerful guardians of the people in their lives. Prima Dona will be designed in Seattle by Dona and made in emerging markets by local tailors and with local fabrics. Dona will start her experiment in Kenya and Nigeria with African fabrics and by independent tailors who are seeking jobs as she has connections in both countries.

For this first version, Dona will work with Leah in Kenya, with the plan to expand to Nigerian tailors next. Dona will design all the garments, have samples made with the specific fabric and photograph the items on real people who are members of the community. Customers will find out about Prima Dona via word-of-mouth, an article or an ad. They will arrive at the website. They will look at the options to order (this will be just 1-3 choices of shapes and prints to start). They will place an order. Dona will review the order and communicate with the customer. Dona will place the order to Leah via text message. Leah will find the right tailor for the job. The tailor will produce the garment. Once a month, Leah will ship a box of garments to Dona (shipping from Kenya is expensive!) who will then individually send them to customers with a hand-written thank you note.

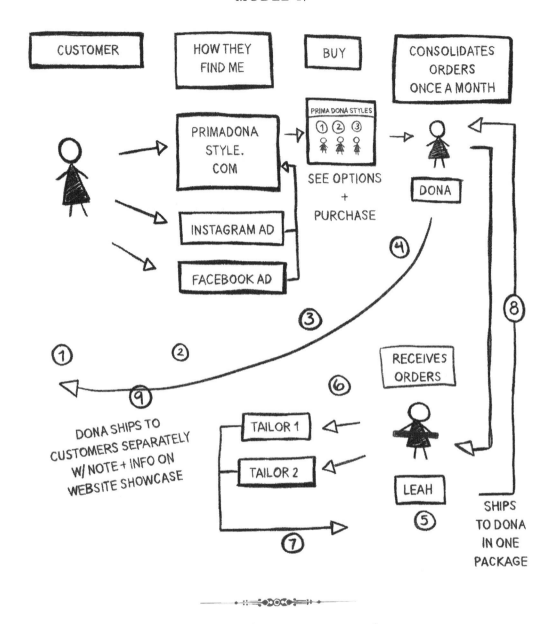

Boxes and Foxes Example

The vision of Boxes and Foxes is to provide high-quality, timely business advice for non-traditional entrepreneurs, who are starting businesses to transform their communities. Boxes and Foxes clients are starting businesses in all industries, everywhere in the world. Jeremiah will offer tailor consulting services to help them solve their specific business questions.

For this first version, Jeremiah will (1) have a basic website explaining what Boxes and Foxes is. Interested clients will (2) fill out a simple request form, explaining who they are and what their business problem is. (3) Jeremiah will use the information gathered from the request form to specially tailor worksheets for exact what the founder's challenge is. Sometimes, the worksheet alone will answer the founder's question. Other times, (4) Jeremiah will set up time for a Skype or phone conversation to go more in-depth on their challenge.

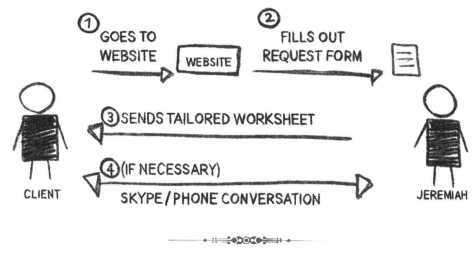

Now it's your turn!

In the workbook, draw your business sketch. You're not making a work of art. Your only objectives are, first, to capture ALL AND ONLY the essential elements of your business and, second, to highlight how these connect with each other. Don't worry if you're not an artist! Dona is, and in her spare time designs fashion using watercolors, creates 3-D holograms, and launches fashion lines. Jeremiah has been told he can't even draw stick figures (which is true). But everyone can do a sketch of their business.

What Is the Competition?

Damilola Samuel discovered one of the great secrets of economic development — ensuring women's education. The young Nigerian entrepreneur impressed us immensely with his desire to tackle one of the most complicated and taboo topics in Nigeria — keeping girls in school during menstruation.

Damilola earned a Computer Science degree from the National Open University of Nigeria. He never expected that degree to lead him down this path. After graduation, he co-founded an organization called Springboard, an agripreneurship organization to help rural youth succeed at farming rather than move into cities and live in poverty (every day we realized more and more how important agriculture is in Nigeria).

Damilola was visiting several farmers in AladeIdanre, a rural community in Southwest Nigeria, trying to help them figure out how to sell their crops better. At one farm, he noticed the farmer's young daughter, Rachel was not at school. He realized he'd seen this trend in a few of the other farms he'd visited. Why were Rachel and other girls not being educated?

As fate would have it, that day on the bus while returning home, he sat next to Ms. Bumi Adeyeyea, a community science teacher. He asked her why so many young girls missed school. Bumi explained how menstruation robs these young rural girls of education. Most rural school girls lack knowledge of menstrual hygiene. Usually they're not aware of sanitary pads because they have never seen one. And even if they are aware, families like Rachel's often can't afford them. Improvised solutions — old towels, rags, paper from notebooks and magazines — often fail, causing infections and embarrassment. Every month, girls would miss four to five days of school. Once hitting puberty, girls dropped further and further behind the boys. Many girls would drop out of school entirely, get impregnated and continue the same cycle of poverty their parents fell under.

Damilola came to believe this issue was holding back more farming communities than most of the other problems he'd seen so far. After researching a bit more, he learned that over 20 million women in rural Nigeria don't use sanitary pads during menstruation. Like Rachel, they'd improvise with alternative solutions. And those methods failed them. Lacking feminine hygiene products, these girls felt ashamed and embarrassed, compounded by cultural taboos surrounding menstruation. According to UNICEF, 1 out of 10 adolescent girls in Africa miss school during menstruation. Most of these girls eventually drop out.

Damilola saw an opportunity. After a bit of experimentation and research on alternative feminine hygiene products being tested in other parts of the world, he discovered that banana plant fiber, readily available as a by-product of banana farms in the area, could be used to locally produce absorbent and inexpensive sanitary pads. While Damilola was not an expert on feminine hygene, he had passion to solve this real and important problem. He surrounded sought out trusted advisors and built partnerships to make it happen.

He made the first batch of pads, and then worked with community teachers such as Bumi to distribute them to 30 girls at Idanre High School and 70 girls at Anglican Grammar School, both in southwest Nigeria. The girls embraced these sanitary pads and the health information Damilola provided. Greenpad Concepts was born.

Since then, Damilola has sold about 23,000 packets of pads and have distributed 8,400 packets for girls from the lowest income regions. He has reached over 50,000 girls and women of reproductive age in rural and semi-urban areas, with reproductive health information and services. The likelihood of young girls from these regions staying in school increased by 50% after Greenpads were introduced to the communities.

Damilola is ensuring the future workforce with his game-changing work. You can find Greenpads on Facebook if you search for GreenPad Concepts.

Like Damiolola, if you've done your job right, you'll be solving a real problem for a real human being. Humans are survivors. Marvelously inventive. They've likely already tried various solutions to their problem. HOWEVER, there's something not quite right about these other solutions. These alternatives are falling short for some reason. That is great news, since it creates an opening for YOUR solution.

Fully understanding how your customers try to solve the problem NOW helps you in several ways. First, you learn who your competition is.

> Sometimes the alternatives your hero is using will surprise you — that's when you realize you didn't even consider these things were your competition!

When you understand WHO your competition is, you can look to see what that competition has done that your hero even knows about it in the first place. Absolutely the best way to understand your competition is to try their product yourself when you can. If that is impossible (like Damilola), have your hero try it and give you honest feedback on their likes/dislikes and WHY.

You'll unearth things like:

ભ Why do people buy that product?
ભ Where is their product sold?
ભ How is it priced?
ભ What are the pros and cons of the product?
ભ How could the product be better, and why isn't it (cost, materials)?

Second, the set of alternatives your hero has tried can shape which aspects of the solution really matter to them:

- ☙ Is it price? Power? Weight?
- ☙ Being organic, local or sustainably-sourced?
- ☙ Do ingredients matter?
- ☙ What about privacy versus convenience?

Third, knowing your competition and your hero's mindset can help you frame WHY YOU'RE BETTER. This is what fancy marketing professors usually call your "differentiator".

What is the problem you're trying to solve?

Let's start with the problem. Look back at your Sh#tty First Draft. Has your EXACT PROBLEM evolved at all (as you worked on the solution sketch, or maybe as you've gotten to understand your hero and their life more)? If so, edit your problem statement and write it in the workbook. If it hasn't changed at all, you're good. Though you may want to add some of the things you've learned about the competitors and the customers.

Do you have a clear idea in mind of the problem you're trying to solve? Let's now think of the range of options available to your hero, as they seek to solve that problem. They have an incredible range of options in front of them, so think freely! Some options that may be *available* to them (but probably not great options) are: 1) they can IGNORE the problem, pretending that it doesn't exist! Or, 2) they can spend a LOT of money on the problem for something that doesn't QUITE work in the way they need it to.

Have a go at writing down what alternatives your customers currently use. Damilola's hero is Rachel. She's a 16-year-old girl living in Adadeldanre. Using Damilola as an example, here are things that Rachel could POTENTIALLY use to solve their problem instead of Greenpads.

1. She could do nothing and just stay home from school during menstruation
2. She could use old towels, leaves or paper
3. She could buy commercial pads (if she can find AND afford them)

Now, your turn. In the workbook, write down the things that your hero could POTENTIALLY use to solve their problem instead of your solution and why. You'll want to answer:

- ☙ Why do people buy these other products?
- ☙ Where are these other products sold?
- ☙ How are they priced?
- ☙ What are the pros and cons of these products?
- ☙ How could these products be better, and why aren't they (cost, materials)?

Second, the set of alternatives your hero has tried can shape which aspects of the solution really matter to them:

- ☙ Is it price? Power? Weight?
- ☙ Being organic, local or sustainably-sourced?
- ☙ Do ingredients matter?
- ☙ What about privacy versus convenience?

Now, think of your solution sketch. Go through each alternative solution and write down the BIGGEST reason that YOUR solution would be better. Yes, your solution probably isn't fully built yet (otherwise you probably wouldn't have read this far into this book). So it may not YET be true that your solution is ALREADY better that your competition. Writing down how you INTEND to be better than your competition can help you prioritize the set of features you'll want to build first; must-have features.

One last note: Remember that being "cheaper" than the competition, unless you're WAY less expensive and intend to ALWAYS be WAY less expensive (because of your pricing strategy, which we'll cover in the next few sections), is not sufficient. You'll want to have a differentiator that's not *merely* "cheaper."

Next up, think of ways that your solution might NOT be as good as something on the market, and why a customer might still choose yours? Is it because it's more local? Is it because of the amazing customer support you offer?

For example, even if Greenpads were less absorbent than commercial pads (or had to be replaced more often), because they are 1/10 of the cost AND made and sold locally, the customers who couldn't afford commercial pads would choose them.

Greenpad Solutions (Locally-Sourced Hygiene Products)

Alternatives

1. *Do nothing and just stay home from school*
   Greenpads is better because: it keeps girls in school
2. *Use towels, leaves or paper*
   Greenpads is better because: they are much more absorbent, durable, and hygienic
3. *Pay for imported commercial pads that people in rural areas can't afford and don't know how to dispose of*
   Greenpads is better because: they are made locally and consistently available, AND they're much cheaper than commercial pads

Prima Dona Example (Ethically-made statement clothing)

Alternatives

1. *Department store* (e.g. Nordstrom)
   Prima Dona is better because: it's much more unique and is a better story (helping create jobs in emerging markets) even if the tailoring is not as high-end.

2. *Independent boutique* (e.g. RH)

   Prima Dona is better because: it's less expensive because they are made-to-order rather than bulk-produced and stored in a physical storefront.

3. *Garment rental* (e.g. Rent The Runway)

   Prima Dona is better because: You get to order the garment in exactly your size and keep it afterwards

4. *Bespoke tailoring (e.g. Kenyan marketplaces)*

   Prima Dona is better because: The customer does not need to travel to, have design skills or do the work to find a reliable tailor

5. *Upcycled/Second-hand* (e.g. Pretty Parlor)

   Prima Dona is better because: it's new, modern and also exactly in your size

---

Boxes and Foxes Example (consulting for non-traditional startup founders)

Alternatives

1. *Internet Searches (e.g. Bing, Google)*

   Boxes and Foxes is better because: it offers a highly-tailored experience for founders that's way easier and way more specific than random internet searches with no reputation

2. *Online, Self-taught Learning (e.g. Coursera, Stanford, YouTube)*

   Boxes and Foxes is better because: it's much more focused, answering a founder's exact question instead of forcing them to take an entire course on a subject

3. *Startup Books (e.g. Model 47, Lean Startup, Zero to One)*

   Boxes and Foxes is better because: it's much more specific. Do to space and audience constraints, even THE BEST STARTUP BOOK IN THE WORLD, M47 ☺ can't fully answer every single question or cover every single nuance. Boxes and Foxes can.

4. *Internet Searches Other name-brand consultants (e.g. McKinsey, BCG, Bain)*

   Boxes and Foxes is better because: Boxes and Foxes is much lighter weight, and much more affordable. In many cases, "the big consultants" won't even touch most startups—and this is certainly true for non-traditional entrepreneurs with great ideas but limited resources

It's your turn again!

In the workbook, for each alternative your hero has, write down why your solution is better keeping in mind:

- Why do people buy this product?
- Where is their product sold?
- How is it priced?
- What are the pros and cons of the product?
- How could the product be better, and why isn't it (cost, materials)?

Second, the set of alternatives your hero has tried can shape which aspects of the solution really matter to them:

- Is it price? Power? Weight?
- Being organic, local or sustainably-sourced?
- Do ingredients matter?
- What about privacy versus convenience?

Also think about your solution — NOT why it's better but why it might not matter (locally made, your reputation, etc)

Market (As If) To One

Gowon isn't a startup founder. He's a farmer, growing corn in a small field in the Bauchi State of Northeast Nigeria. Droughts are common there, so one of his biggest challenges is getting enough water to irrigate his crops. Several times each season, Gowon needs to pump water up from the muddy river flowing a short distance from his field. If rain doesn't fall and Gowon can't figure out how to get water to his crops, he and his family might starve. Water is THAT important to him.

He's in luck, though. Also living in Northeastern Nigeria, Ibrahim Mohammed Aboki is one of our fellows. As you recall, Ibrahim started the company Basmalah Enterprises to deliver solar-powered irrigation to farmers.

Gowon is the perfect hero for Ibrahim — but Gowon is just one person. To run a profitable business, Ibrahim can't sell ONLY to Gowon. Ibrahim needs to sell a LOT of his solar-powered irrigation solutions. There's no way Gowon could ever buy them all. But neither can Ibrahim sell to every single person in the world. Not all 7.6 billion people globally really need solar-powered irrigation — we, in Seattle, Washington don't, for example.

What Ibrahim needs to do is find a lot of people LIKE Gowon, who would also benefit from his product. Ibrahim knows they exist. Like Gowon, about a third of the Nigerian labor force works in agriculture. More than nine in 10 of Nigerian farmers are small-holders, like Gowon. They can find it difficult to scrape together the money to buy petrol-powered generators to water their fields. Even if they buy or borrow a pump, the petrol to fuel that pump can fluctuate dramatically in price, unpredictably decreasing the farmer's profit and production.

To run a profitable business, our founders needed to sub-divide the world into "people like Gowon" and "people not like Gowon."

There is a decent chance that people like Gowon *might* buy solar-powered irrigation. People NOT like Gowon won't. That, team, is marketing. Find the Gowons. Let's do that.

What Makes A Person "Gowon-Like?"

In the previous chapter, we explained that Ibrahim needs to figure out who in the world is like Gowon. Let's first make an admission. We were simplifying. Gowon-like folk may not be the ONLY people in the world who'd want solar-powered irrigation. There might be a woman named Meta, leading the irrigation team for a large corporation named the Kereksuk Rice Producers (KRP) in Laos. Meta at KRP is not at all like Gowon, but that does not mean she couldn't potentially use solar powered irrigation in several of her inland rice paddies. Maybe John, growing organic wines in the foothills of Temecula, California, would be interested in solar-powered irrigation, too.

Remember, though, Ibrahim's hero is Gowon. To ensure that he's truly solving a real problem for a real person, it will help him to co-create with that real person, then generalize characteristics outwards to a customer segment. As a founder with limited resources and time, Ibrahim will start by building for one — initially for one actual person, and then as time goes on, for one group of people with similar characteristics to that individual. Eventually, Ibrahim might choose to build for several heroes, each representing the views of different consumer segments: Meta in Laos, John in Temecula. Each hero, and each segment, might require a slightly different product, message, or value prop. But first Ibrahim will start with one person, and build outwards. Right now, he's looking for "Gowon-like people."

But what does "like Gowon" mean? What essential characteristics of Gowon can help Ibrahim track down people like him? Using these characteristics, we could divide up the world into people who share these traits. People at fancy business schools call this process of divvying up the world "segmentation".

According to Ibrahim, there are a LOT of characteristics to choose from. Gowon is 32 years old, male, and of a lower socio-economic bracket. He dropped out of high school. He's literate but doesn't read very much. He lives outside Azare in the rural north of Nigeria. Gowon belongs to the Hausa tribe. He speaks Hausa and a bit of English. He sees himself as a provider for a large household. In addition to his wife and five children, his adult mother and father live with him. Gowon describes himself as dependable, careful with the limited resources he owns. He's a farmer. He grows corn. He spends nearly every day in his field — clearing the earth, sowing seeds, watering, removing pests, and harvesting. Gowon is Muslim, and when he's not in the fields he goes frequently to the mosque. Occasionally, Gowon attends his local farmer's association meetings.

Understanding our hero like this helps us refine our decisions. Like every other human being, Gowon is complex. To generalize the actual person Gowon into "Gowon-like characteristics," we can use four main categories of variables: their *geography*, their *demographics*, their *behaviors*, and their *psychographics*. In seeking to understand the characteristics of your hero, you can choose one of these, all of them, or as many as you think are relevant to the definition.

Geographic variables are based largely on where your potential customers live and work. Do they live in a city or more of a rural area? Do they all live in one single town? One single state? One single country? A continent? In cold places? Deserts? Geo variables can be important for products sold for similar climate ranges (e.g. products such as umbrellas, sunscreen, wool coats, and skis) and for products based on urban vs suburban living (e.g. products for those who drive to work [such as new tires or a roof rack] vs walk to work [such as sneakers or backpacks]). Another scenario where geographic (geo) segmentation is important is for businesses with a physical location (e.g. coffee shops and grocery stores), or a relatively limited ability to reach customers (for example, lawn-mowing services and babysitters have a much smaller geographic reach than a book, smartphone app, or movie). Location is important to Ibrahim, since his small business can't yet service the entire country of Nigeria.

Demographic variables include characteristics such as a person's age, gender, and nationality (which is more than geo: there are Nigerians living worldwide, for example). Other variables include their religion, race, ethnicity, level of education, income, marital status, family size, and occupation. You can also use demographic variables if you're looking to sell to businesses (business-to-business, also referred to as B2B) vs selling only to consumers (business-to-consumer, which stands for B2C). For B2B demographics, you'll think about where your hero works. What is the size of their company? What industry? What is their job/function? How long have they been working there? Some demographics will be important to Ibrahim, since the service he's selling would really only be interesting to other farmers like Gowon.

Behavioral variables come from what people tend to do; the actions they tend to take. What other products do they already use? Which teams or political parties or music groups do they support? What occasions (e.g. birthdays, anniversaries and holidays) do they celebrate? What games do they play? What are their favorite sports? What are their modes of transportation? Ibrahim might be able to use some behavioral factors, as well. For example, he'll only be able to attract people who take the action of watering their fields.

Psychographic variables describe aspects of your hero's lifestyle, values, social class, and personality. How do they describe themselves? For example, someone who calls themself a "caregiver." A "thrill-seeker." "Dependable." "Fun-loving."

Often, psychographic features are hidden; they aren't super obvious. That doesn't make psychographic variables any less valuable, though! Nor is it impossible to uncover them. In some cases, you can use people's behaviors as a proxy for their psychographics. For example, you might want to consider people who are "budget conscious." Some of the behaviors we could use as a proxy for "budget conscious" are clipping coupons, negotiating, delaying purchases to await sales, and using apps or websites to compare prices.

By using these segmentation factors to identify consumers, we can look for traits these other people share with our hero.

For example, Ibrahim knows his target customers will be farmers like Gowon. But should Ibrahim target all farmers? All male farmers? All Northern Nigerian farmers? All Nigerian farmers who are Hausa? All farmers who harvest? All corn farmers? All Nigerian corn farmers who are male?

Some of these characteristics aren't super important in isolation. Most, but not all, Nigerian farmers are male. Many, but certainly not all, farmers in Northern Nigeria grow corn. All farmers — regardless of gender or crop — spend their time clearing the earth, sowing seeds, removing pests, and harvesting. So it's not super useful to use EVERY one of Gowon's traits to look for people LIKE Gowon. We only need "close enough." Ibrahim would almost certainly want to sell solar-powered irrigation to cassava farmers. To female farmers. To people belonging to ethnic groups other than Hausa.

Therefore, we need to figure out which characteristics have the most impact on how we'd market our product. If Ibrahim uses Gowon as the basis for his segmentation, the characteristics he'd look at might include the following:

Demographic

- ⚬ Farmer
- ⚬ Head of large household
- ⚬ 32 years old
- ⚬ Male
- ⚬ Lower socio-economic class
- ⚬ High school dropout
- ⚬ Literate
- ⚬ Belongs to the Hausa tribe

Geographic

- ⚬ Lives in Northeastern Nigeria

Behavioral

     ርჳ Owns a small field

     ርჳ Grows corn

     ርჳ Married with children

     ርჳ Speaks Hausa and some English

Psychographic

     ርჳ Describes himself as dependable, careful, and hard-working

In your workbook, write down everything you can think of that might be relevant to your hero. Think about their geography, their demographics, their behaviors, and their psychographics. Write these in the Criterion column.

Above, we wrote down some 14 characteristics. Of course, there are more, but that's good enough for now. Now, let's consider each one and assign it a priority (High, Medium, and Low) and a "Why?", which describes how useful that characteristic might be to people who would pay for that product.

Criterion	Priority	Why?
Demographics: Occupation (Gowon is a farmer)	High	Basmalah's service is optimized to deliver solar-powered irrigation to farmers who grow crops that require water. Even other people who work in agriculture but don't grow crops (like shepherds, people who raise poultry or cattle) wouldn't be a great customer for Basmalah's services.

Criterion	Priority	Why?
Demographics: Size of field (Small field, Medium-sized field, Large field)	Medium	Size of field could be a good proxy for 1) a farmer's ability to pay for the service -- larger fields typically mean larger harvests and higher revenues, and 2) a farmer's need for irrigation (larger fields mean more area to water)
Demographics: Type of crop: corn, beans, cassava, cocoa beans, groundnuts, melon, millet, palm kernels, palm oil, plantains, rice, rubber, sorghum, soybeans, bananas and yams	Medium	Different crops have varying water needs over their growing periods. For example, beans need 300-500mm of water over their total growing period. Corn (maize) requires 500-800mm. It might make sense to prioritize the farmers of crops more dependent on water.
Geography: Northern Nigeria, Southern Nigeria, Eastern Nigeria, Western Nigeria, Northeastern Nigeria, All Nigeria	High	Geographic focus can help Basmalah market and distribute their product (for example, if roads are better in the South than in the North, or farmers' co-operatives are more prevalent), or more farms in that area grow crops that need more irrigation. More tactically, Basmalah Enterprises is based in Northeastern Nigeria. For the moment, all of its employees and equipment is there. Serving customers in another region would be difficult at this stage of their business.
Demographics: Family size (Unmarried, Married no children, Married with Children)	Low	Potentially farmers who are married with children are more likely to be interested in services that have a more stable cost structure.

Criterion	Priority	Why?
Demographics: Primary language (There are over 520 languages spoken in Nigeria. In addition to English, some of the most common languages are: Hausa, Igbo, Yoruba, Urhobo, Ibibio, Edo, Fulfulde, Kanuri, and Igala)	Medium	While it is sometimes easier to develop marketing materials in a single language (which in Nigeria would usually be English), people respond better to communication in their own native tongue (which in Nigeria would vary according to a person's region and tribe).
Demographics: Literate, Not Literate	Medium	Basmalah Enterprises needs to communicate with farmers, for example to explain why they would pay for solar-powered irrigation of their field. While it's true that it'd be easiest for Ibrahim's team to market to farmers through methods that require literacy (flyers in feed stores, ads in newspapers or on Facebook, and the like), it would also be possible to pick other communications methods that don't need as much literacy—like word-of-mouth, radio ads, and possibly even TV ads.
Demographics: Age (32 years old), Sex (Male), Education (High-School dropout), Religion (Islam)	Low	These characteristics most likely are not super relevant to Gowon's need to water his fields.
Demographics: Socio-Economic Class (lower class, middle-class, upper-class)	Medium	Relevant insofar as potential customers can afford the services Basmalah Enterprises offer (which will depend on their price)

Criterion	Priority	Why?
Psychographics: Describe themselves as "Dependable," "Careful," and "Hardworking"	Low	While Psychographic characteristics can be useful in HOW we market to a group of people, in this case it can be difficult at a glance to figure out which people share these beliefs, and which don't.
Behavioral: clear the earth, sow seeds, water field, remove pests, harvest, irrigate farm, attend mosque	Low	While Behavioral characteristics can be useful in HOW we market to a group of people, in this case most of the behaviors we care about (irrigate crops, harvest crops, etc) are captured by the Demographic "occupation."

Prima Dona Example

For Prima Dona, the Gowans will be quite different—busy professionals who tend to travel and have side-hustles but the same exercise works great.

Criterion	Priority	Why?
Demographics: Occupation – professional	Med	Prima Dona's designs will be optimized for people who are business professionals but anyone can buy them
Demographic: Women	Low	Prima Dona is being designed with a woman in mind and the marketing is going to be targeted to women, but anyone can wear the garments
Psychographic: Believes in giving back	Med	Prima Dona will have a social impact angle

Criterion	Priority	Why?
Psychographic: Is not afraid to be noticed	High	The clothing will also be noticeable and different than the usual in professional environments
Psychographic: must be flexible	High	Because Prima Dona is made to order, they will not receive their garment the next day — and they might never receive exactly what they ordered if we run out of fabric — they will be issued a refund in this case
Behavioral: Buys fashion on-line	High	Prima Dona will be sold almost exclusively online

Boxes and Foxes Example

For Boxes and Foxes, the Gowans will be somewhere in the middle. Both people in developed and emerging markets with some ability to pay for a consulting service

Criterion	Priority	Why?
Demographic: Women, 30+ years old, American, married, mother, Masters Degree	Low	Boxes and Foxes is optimized for any founder, regardless of gender, age, nationality, marital or parental status, or education level
Geographic: Lives in an urban area (in this case, Amsterdam)	Low	Boxes and Foxes is optimized for any founder, regardless of location. However, they need to have internet connectivity to communicate with me and also to be able to implement the recommendations.
Psychographic: Warrior, self-reliant	Med	Boxes and Foxes' ideal client believes they can overcome any challenge, even if they don't quite know how to do it yet.

Criterion	Priority	Why?
Behavioral: Startup founder	High	Boxes and Foxes will be most useful for founders who are able to pay for advice but are unable (yet) to pay for a full-time employee with these skills.
Behavioral: Willing to outsource	High	Boxes and Foxes will be most useful for founders who are able to focus on the core parts of the business while relying on outside experts for the more tactical, one-off (but important) tasks.

Now, in your workbook, circle the criteria that you think are the most important for your heroes. These are likely going to be all the ones you marked as "High" importance.

Pick "Gowon-Like" People

Remember, the entire reason we look for "people like Gowon" is that we ultimately need to sell to a large group of people. We want to sell to the "people who are like Gowon," not the "people unlike Gowon." We may get lucky, and a few "people unlike Gowon" might buy from us — but they'll be the exception, not the rule. We're building for, and marketing to, one "type" of person: Gowon.

But, like every other human being, Gowon is complicated. We could describe him in many ways. How can we use the "essentially Gowon" characteristics to decide which group of people we want to sell to? Which group do we want to target?

TARGETING = FIND MORE PEOPLE LIKE YOUR HERO

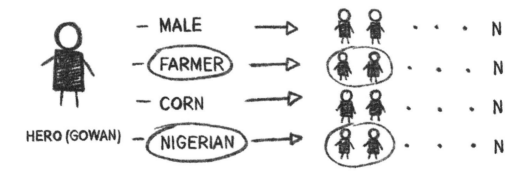

There are two main features that matter most to us as we search for a group to target. First, is the group profitable enough? Can we survive as a business by targeting that group of people? Are there enough people in that group, and are they willing to spend enough money for us to stay in business? Second, assuming the group is profitable enough, will they be willing to buy *our* product (considering all the potential alternatives they could select, as well as the strengths of our product, company, and brand)? We need a "yes" answer to both questions.

Trying to figure out the answer to the first question isn't rocket science. Are there enough people in our target group for us to be profitable? Fancy MBAs call this figuring out your "Total Addressable Market," or TAM. For selling solar-powered irrigation, the critical characteristic for Ibrahim is that "people like Gowon" be crop farmers (their crops need water to grow). There are lots of crop farmers in Nigeria, so the TAM is large. Of course, Ibrahim would never be able to sell to EVERY SINGLE ONE of these people, but knowing your TAM is a helpful benchmark to understanding the maximum number of customers you potentially could ever have.

We could spend some time quantifying its size. How many Nigerian farmers are there? According to figures from the Nigerian Ministry of Statistics, roughly *a third of Nigeria's labor force works in agriculture. Nigeria's labor force was about 60 million* in 2017. So, assuming that the percentage of farmers hasn't changed too much between 2014 and 2017, we can estimate that the TAM for *"all Nigerian farmers" is about 20 million.*

A second, but also super important, characteristic for Ibrahim is that potential customers have their farms in Northeastern Nigeria (specifically Bauchi State) since that's where all of Ibrahim's employees live, and his equipment is situated. Not all the Nigerian crop farmers live in Bauchi State, so Ibrahim's TAM shrinks a bit, but it's still a large number. We're not spending a lot of time getting exact numbers, but we do want to understand if we have a decent-sized target population. Wikipedia lists Nigerian states by their population (based on the Nigeria census of 2006), which estimates that Bauchi state represents about *3% of the total population of Nigeria.* Using a very quick calculation with a bunch of assumptions, *3% of 20 million people is about 60,000 people* — so the rough TAM of "Nigerian farmers in Bauchi state" is **60,000 people**.

We're doing this quickly. We spent about 20 minutes on the internet to find three numbers — the Nigerian labor market size, percentage of the Nigerian labor market in agriculture, and the Nigerian population breakdown by state. Clearly, we could spend more time to find estimates with a higher likelihood of accuracy. However, for now we only want to help Ibrahim understand whether a lot of people might share the same problem Gowon has (a need to water their fields), and because of that would EVER pay for solar powered irrigation. Answer? Yes. To Ibrahim, 60,000 people is a lot of potential customers.

Ibrahim can also potentially leverage some of Gowon's other characteristics to get even more granular with his targeting. Here are three potential options among the many he could use:

- He could target marketing at small-holder farmers. Perhaps Ibrahim could run a campaign that highlights solar-powered irrigation as a "Gowon vs Goliath" tool, to help small-holder farmers in Bauchi state feel like they can access some of the same resources that bigger operations use.
- He could target marketing at members of the Hausa tribe. Maybe Ibrahim could target farmers in Bauchi state who belong to the same tribe he does, suggesting that he understands their challenges and concerns well since he is one of them.
- He could target marketing at corn farmers. Ibrahim could consider targeting only one type of crop grown by Nigerian farmers in Bauchi state, and create marketing that focuses on the needs of this specific group.

Each option brings with it some trade-offs.

The more specific and you are with our customer, the more precisely you can market your product. At the same time, the more specific you are, the smaller your potential market size.

Ultimately, Ibrahim chose to focus on the broader group of "all Nigerian farmers living in Bauchi state" as his target.

Remember, calculating your TAM is very loose. You only want to ensure that there are enough people (and enough revenue) in the segment you're targeting, to be worthwhile. If you're TOO specific with your target, you simply won't be profitable. Since it's nearly impossible to get super close to the exact number, we're not going to spend too much time here. But it is important to have a rough idea of how big a total addressable market you can be going after. Let's take a look at our two example businesses, to get an idea how to do this.

Prima Dona Example

According to our work in the previous chapter, here are the ideal characteristics for the ideal consumer for Prima Dona. They are people who:

- Are willing to buy their fashion online
- Are willing to make a "statement" in the clothes they wear
- Are able to be "flexible" on when their order arrives, since it may take a bit of time for their Prima Dona garments to be delivered

Let's take them one at a time. First, to estimate the number of people willing to buy their fashion online, we typed these words into our search engine: "What % of people buy clothes online?" (We told you it wasn't that hard ☺) Now, the trick is to make sense of the search results. According to the results we got, just on the first page, the % of people who would buy online could be 49%, 70%, or 79%. OR (much more likely), the number isn't ANY of these. But how to decide? Since our intent is to do this quickly, we're simply going to take the lowest number (and call ourselves "conservative.") We think that 49% is a bit *too* specific, and we don't really know. So let's just call *the percentage of people willing to purchase online 50%*.

So it turns out that we can actually search for the % of people who would buy their clothes online. Unfortunately, it's not nearly so easy to figure out what search terms to use for the % of people willing to make a statement, or the % of people who are willing to be flexible on delivery time. To some extent, it'd be very difficult (ok impossible) to estimate these figures…so for now, we're totally going to make them up (and get better as we go forward with our business.

As Dona thinks about a typical 100 people that she knows, she would guess that not many of them would be willing to make a statement. Most people, she'd guess, would rather feel safer wearing muted colors like earth tones, greys, blacks, and other colors that more or less "blend in." Maybe 1 person out of every 5 (Dona guesses) is willing to make a statement. Fine – let's use this number. Let's call the *% of people who'd be willing to make a statement in their fashion 20%*.

It'd also be pretty difficult, as we sit here in this coffeeshop, to estimate with any degree of accuracy the percentage of people who would be willing to be flexible on their delivery time. We could make the number up, like the previous figure. Or, we could see if anyone's ever done a similar calculation before. We looked online for this phrase: "what percentage of people would be willing to wait a bit longer for their delivery time." To our surprise, on the first page of search results, we found a report entitled "Ecommerce delivery: what do customers want?" The report included a chart summarizing their research (a survey of 1,000 online respondents), which had the question "Thinking about delivery options, what would make you more likely to buy online?" 30% of respondents said "a fixed delivery date" as their top option. We could use the inverse of that, to estimate that *70% of people would be a bit more flexible on their delivery time*.

So now we have the numbers we were looking for. They're not perfect, but they'll do for now.

Are willing to buy their fashion online: **50%**

Are willing to make a "statement" in the clothes they wear: **20%**

Are able to be "flexible" on when their order arrives, since it may take a bit of time for their Prima Dona garments to be delivered: **70%**

We're looking for the number of people this would describe. Although we could use a BIG number, like the population of the world (~7.4 billion people), let's again be "conservative" and look at the population of the United States, initially: **327 million people**

So, to calculate our rough TAM, we'd multiply these numbers together:

TAM = (US population) x (% buy online) x (% make a statement) x (% flexible delivery)

TAM = 327 million x 50% x 20% x 70%

TAM = about 23 million people (in the US alone)

Boxes and Foxes Example

Now we've got the process down. Let's move quickly to estimate the TAM for Boxes and Foxes. Looking at our work in the previous chapter, Jeremiah will use two main dimensions to identify his target. His target audience for Boxes and Foxes will be:

- ☙ Startup founders
- ☙ Willing to outsource the answers to focused business questions

Initially, to help make his TAM a bit easier, Jeremiah will focus on finding numbers in the US (even though his clients are already global).

To estimate the % of people who are startup founders, Jeremiah typed this phrase into a search engine: "How many entrepreneurs in the United States?" The very first search result pointed Jeremiah to an article by INC, containing this quote: "A new report from the Global Entrepreneurship Monitor (GEM), sponsored by Babson College and Baruch College, finds that *27 million working-age Americans--nearly 14 percent--are starting or running new businesses.*"

Next, Jeremiah needs to estimate the % of startup founders who'd be willing to outsource finding the answers to specific business questions. To truly get a good idea of this number, he'd need to run his own survey. Remember, though, he's currently sitting in a coffeeshop TRYING TO FINISH THE TAM CHAPTER. So, there's not enough time right now to send out a survey to a bunch of entrepreneurs. He'll use the tried and true method of TOTALLY MAKING UP the percentage. Based on his experience of working with startup founders, he's noticed that they're a relatively pragmatic group of people. As long as they're getting a good value exchange, they're focused on #DoingTheThing. Jeremiah thinks that about 9 out of every 10 startup founders would outsource to a good business consultant. So, he'll estimate that *90% of startup founders would outsource.*

To calculate our rough TAM, we'd multiply these numbers together:

TAM = (US startup founders) x (% willing to outsource)

TAM = 27 million x 90%

TAM = about 24 million people (in the US alone)

Let's be very clear. We are not implying in any way that you shouldn't try to find the best numbers you can, in order to estimate the size of your target group. Being able to aim your business at a VERY big group of potential buyers is a super important idea.

Our point is only that, it can be difficult and sometimes expensive to get TOO close in your estimates. Since it's difficult and or expensive to get too close to the number, our suggestion is that you ACKNOWLEDGE that you don't really know the exact size with any real confidence.

In the early days, however, this doesn't really matter. Using just our three examples—

- ✆ There is no way, right now, that Ibrahim could actually irrigate the fields for all 60,000 farmers he estimates as his TAM
- ✆ There is no way, right now, that Dona could provide with garments all 23 million people she estimates as her TAM
- ✆ There is no way, right now, that Jeremiah could provide focused, highly-tailored business advice to 24 million people he estimates as his TAM

So, we'll call these TAMs "good enough," and keep moving ☺

Now, do the same in your workbook. Considering the prioritized traits of your hero, what group of customers do you want to target? Can you do a quick estimate of the size of that group (your TAM)? (Don't spend a ton of time on this task – the idea is to have a VERY high-level understanding of how many people you're talking about.)

Fit Your Solution into Gowon's World

Since we've figured out "who's like Gowon," now we just market to them. Simple, right? Not quite. In the fancy MBA model of "Segmentation, Targeting, and Positioning," we're now ready to position our product in our target's mind.

Positioning is the art of building — and communicating — a solution that lies squarely in the "right spot" for how our target group understands the problem we're solving, for how our solution might fit into their life, and for why they'd choose *our* solution instead of some other alternative.

> If we do our job right, our product's position will help our target audience "get" what our product does to improve their life, and why they should use our product, instead of something else.

Of course, if you're reading M47 at the right place in your product development, you don't *have* a product yet. That's actually perfect! Before spending lots of time building and marketing something, we want to understand the ways in which we want our customers to perceive our product, both versus the solution we're solving, and versus our competition.

Making a Perceptual Map

Fancy MBAs call the process of fitting your product into the factors important to your hero "making a perceptual map." To do make a perceptual map, you follow this process:

1. Write down the factors most important to your hero, when evaluating potential solutions to their problem
2. Pick the two MOST IMPORTANT factors, then draw them on a graph (like an x / y graph from old-school math)
3. Take a look at where, across those factors, your competition lies, and put them on the graph (err, perceptual map)
4. Now, place your own product where you'd *want* it to be on the map. (If your product is already being sold, there may be a difference between where you'd *want* it to be, and where your consumers *think it actually is* right now — it's totally fine to put BOTH positions on the map)

To do step one, we need to identify the dimensions of potential solutions to your hero's problem. How do people *choose among* solutions?

Perceptual Map Step #1: Write down the important dimensions

As the people in your target audience think about ways to solve their problem, what are the aspects of the solution that are most relevant to them? Let's consider both functional and emotional dimensions.

- ଔ Functional dimensions are factual things like the cost of the solution, the weight, color or size.
- ଔ Emotional dimensions are how a solution makes your hero feel. You can influence these through things like using premium or one-of-a-kind materials, advertising that's tailored to your hero, or great customer service.

Here are three examples, from companies we've discussed earlier:

Basmalah Enterprises (Solar-Powered Irrigation)

Functional Dimensions (characteristics of the solution)

- *Cost*: "I'd prefer an irrigation solution that is inexpensive" vs "I'd prefer an irrigation solution that does the job well (even if it costs slightly more)"
- *Ownership*: "I'd prefer an irrigation solution that I own fully" vs "I'd prefer an irrigation solution that I rent only when I need it"

Emotional Dimensions (how the solution makes your hero feel)

- *Innovation:* "I'd prefer an irrigation solution that makes me feel open to new methods" vs "I'd prefer an irrigation solution that makes me feel traditional"
- *Environmentalism:* "I'd prefer an irrigation solution that makes me feel green" (takes care of the earth)" vs "I'd prefer an irrigation solution that makes me feel highly-effective" (to get my crops watered)"

Prima Dona (Ethically Made Statement Fashion)

Functional Dimensions (characteristics of the solution)

- *Cost:* "I'd prefer a garment that is inexpensive" vs "I'd prefer a garment that is premium"
- *Versatility:* "I'd prefer a garment that is single occasion" vs "I'd prefer a garment that is all-occasion"
- *Availability:* "I'd prefer a garment that is available anywhere vs "I'd prefer a garment that is niche"
- *Season:* "I'd prefer a garment that is timeless" vs "I'd prefer a garment that is on-trend"
- *Palette:* "I'd prefer a garment that is muted" vs "I'd prefer a garment that is statement"
- *Sourcing:* "I'd prefer a garment that is brand-name vs "I'd prefer a garment that is high-impact (helps the people who craft it)"

Emotional Dimensions (how the solution makes your hero feel)

- ❦ *Power:* "I'd prefer a garment that makes me feel elegant and understated" vs "I'd prefer a garment that makes me feel bold"
- ❦ *Uniqueness:* "I'd prefer a garment that helps me fit in" vs "I'd prefer a garment that helps me stand out"

Boxes and Foxes (Business advice for non-traditional founders)

Functional Dimensions (characteristics of the solution)

- ❦ *Customization:* "I'd prefer consulting that is tailored to my individual needs" vs "I'd prefer consulting that is standard across industries and specifics"
- ❦ *Cost:* "I'd prefer consulting that fits my budget" vs "I'd prefer consulting that solves my exact problem (even if it costs a little more)"

Emotional Dimensions (how the solution makes your hero feel)

- ❦ *Recognition:* "I'd prefer consulting that has name-brand reputation" vs "I'd prefer consulting recommended by others like me"
- ❦ *Human touch:* "I'd prefer consulting that makes me feel personally respected and valued" vs "I'd prefer consulting that's very formal and traditional"

Perceptual Map Step #2: Write down the dimensions most important to your hero

Now, pick the two most important dimensions (ideally one functional, and one emotional). Draw two intersecting lines. The vertical axis represents the functional; the horizontal axis represents the emotional.

Basmalah Enterprises (Solar-Powered Irrigation)

Functional

- ❧ *Cost:* "I'd prefer an irrigation solution that is inexpensive" vs "I'd prefer an irrigation solution that does the job well (even if it costs slightly more)"
- ❧ *Innovation:* "I'd prefer an irrigation solution that makes me feel open to new methods" vs "I'd prefer an irrigation solution that makes me feel traditional"

Prima Dona (Ethically Made Statement Fashion)

Functional

- ❧ *Season:* "I'd prefer a garment that is timeless" vs "I'd prefer a garment that is on-trend"

Emotional

- ❧ *Uniqueness:* "I'd prefer a garment that helps me fit in" vs "I'd prefer a garment that helps me stand out"

Boxes and Foxes (Business advice for non-traditional founders)

Functional

- ❧ *Cost:* "I'd prefer consulting that fits my budget" vs "I'd prefer consulting that solves my exact problem (even if it costs a little more)"

Emotional (how the solution makes your hero feel)
- ❧ *Recognition:* "I'd prefer consulting that has name-brand reputation" vs "I'd prefer consulting recommended by others like me"

Perceptual Map Steps #3 & 4: Place your competitors (and your product) on the map

Now, we want to look at our competition, and determine where they would lie, according to those dimensions. For each of the three businesses we're looking at, here are their main alternatives / competitors.

Basmalah Enterprises (Solar-Powered Irrigation)

Alternatives

1. *Petrol-powered Irrigation*
2. *Hope it rains*

Prima Dona (Ethically Made Statement Fashion)

Alternatives

1. *Department store* (e.g. Nordstrom)
2. *Independent boutique* (e.g. Luly Wang)
3. *Garment rental* (e.g. Armoire, Rent The Runway)
4. *Clothing boxes* (e.g. Trunk Club, StitchFix)
5. *Bespoke tailoring* (e.g. Kenyan marketplaces)
6. *Upcycled/Second-hand* (e.g. Pretty Parlor)

Boxes and Foxes (Business advice for non-traditional founders)

Alternatives

1. *Internet Searches (e.g. Bing, Google)*
2. *Online, Self-taught Learning (e.g. Coursera, Stanford, YouTube)*
3. *Startup Books (e.g. Model 47, Lean Startup, Zero to One)*
4. *Other name-brand consultants (e.g. McKinsey, BCG, Bain)*

Here's where these competitors (alternatives) fall on the perceptual map.

Basmalah Enterprises (Solar-Powered Irrigation)

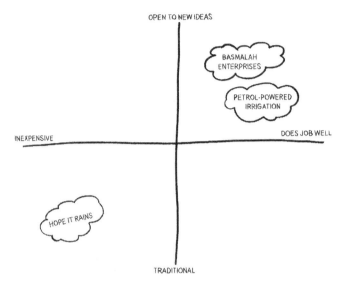

Prima Dona (Ethically Made Statement Fashion)

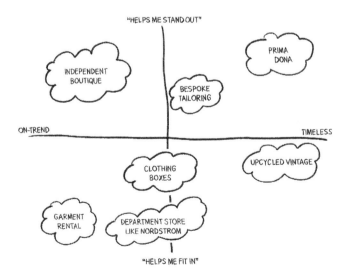

Boxes and Foxes (Business advice for non-traditional founders)

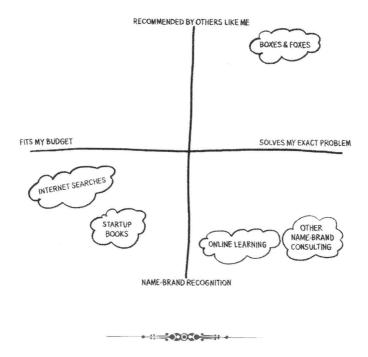

Now, do the same in your workbook. Draw your own perceptual map!

1. Write down the dimensions most important to your hero, when evaluating potential solutions to their problem
2. Pick the two MOST IMPORTANT dimensions, then draw them on a graph (like an x / y graph from old-school math)
3. Take a look at where, across those dimensions, your competition lies, and put them on the graph (err, perceptual map)
4. Now, place your own product where you'd want it to be on the map. (If your product is already being sold, there may be a difference between where you'd want it to be, and where your consumers think it actually is right now — it's totally fine to put BOTH positions on the map)

MODEL 47

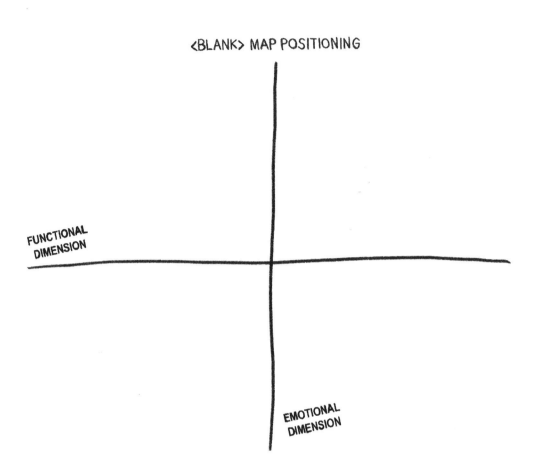

<BLANK> MAP POSITIONING

FUNCTIONAL
DIMENSION

EMOTIONAL
DIMENSION

State Your Value Proposition

For Nigerian Law School students, Lawcademy makes studying law easier than other instructional materials by making lessons simpler and more fun.

Your value proposition (what we usually call a value prop) is one of the most important statements for your business that you'll come up with. You'll use it over and over, and over again. You'll use it on potential customers, partners, suppliers, and of course with your family when you try to explain what you do all day. It spells out your business in ONE sentence.

This sentence is called a Value Prop. This is a VERY short summary of:

- ❧ Who is your customer?
- ❧ What is your solution to their problem?
- ❧ What is your competitive advantage?
- ❧ Who are your key competitors?

For <customer>, <your business>
<does what> <how better> than
<key competitors>,
<how>.

Yes, we know that makes little sense. Let's break into down using the value props of some of our entrepreneurs you've hopefully become familiar with.

Entrepreneur	Dr. Moses	Damilola	Ibrahim
For Customer	Pregnant women	Rural girls	Farmers in Northeastern Nigeria
Your Business	SonoCare	Greenpad	Basmalah
Does What	Identifies high-risk pregnancies	Keeps them in school during their menstrual period	Pumps water
How Better	More convenient, affordable and accurate	Health education and lower-cost products	Less expensively
Competitors	Expensive, remote, understaffed/under-equipped clinics	Unhygienic or expensive products	Petrol-consuming generators
How	By providing mobile diagnostic medical imaging services	By providing health education and lower cost biodegradable sanitary pads	By using mobile solar power

Dr. Moses's value prop in sentence form:

For pregnant women, SonoCare identifies high-risk pregnancies better than expensive, remote, understaffed, and underequipped clinics by providing convenient, affordable, and accurate testing through mobile diagnostic medical imaging services.

Damilola's value prop in sentence form:

GreenPad Concepts helps rural girls stay in school during their menstrual period, versus unhygienic or expensive products, by providing health education and low cost, biodegradable sanitary pads.

Ibrahim's value prop in sentence form:

For Nigerian farmers, Basmalah Enterprises pumps water less expensively than petrol-consuming generators, by using mobile solar power.

Dona's value prop in sentence form:

For AND people, Prima Dona offers 'statement clothing for all aspects of your life' more ethically than mainstream shops and boutiques, through a made-to-order process creating jobs for emerging market tailors.

Jeremiah's value prop in sentence form:

Boxes and Foxes provides business advice for non-traditional startup founders better than online learning, startup books, and traditional consultants — by offering highly-customized consulting services recommended by people like you.

Your turn to now

Do this in the workbook. Don't worry about getting it 100% accurate the first time. Ours are still not that great yet. It took almost a week for our entrepreneurs to finalize theirs.

List Your Assumptions

They showed up with powdered cowpeas in a plastic bag. Turned out they'd been doing that all over Nigeria for months.

Many of our entrepreneurs are solving a problem for someone else. Kido Chukwunweike and Kelechi Odoemena, however, are solving a problem for themselves. A few years ago, Kido was away at grad school in the United Kingdom (UK). He yearned for his mother's Nigerian home cooking. He dreamt of akara bean cakes — a classic breakfast dish made of cowpeas (beans) that were ground up, made into cakes and pan-fried with spicy chilis and onions. (We ate this every morning in Lagos and yes, it's as delicious as it sounds). Typically, making these bean cakes takes nearly two hours, since cowpeas need to be cleaned, soaked, peeled and then milled. For Kido, there was little chance he could make akara bean cakes given his busy schedule as a grad student. One day, Kido's Nigerian roommate received a care package from his family, which included a packet of powdered cowpeas. The powder was made by his roommate's mother, so her son could easily make his favorite Nigerian food in less than 20 minutes. Though cowpeas are a staple of the Nigerian diet, Kido wondered why they simply weren't available in processed form. Local cowpea farmers lacked this substantial business opportunity.

Kido, with a background in supply chain logistics, started thinking. He had an idea but he needed help. He reached out to his longtime friend Kelechi Odoemena. Kelechi focused on agricultural economics and had extensive experience in operations— he'd worked on everything from fish farms to vegetable crops. They concocted the idea of making and selling processed cowpeas that cooked in 20 minutes — giving time back to Nigerians without sacrificing the comforts of home cooking. Using safe, chemical-free processing and creating a market for farmers, Kido and Kelechi work to strengthen farmers' livelihoods and economic security in Nigeria.

Today, Dilish Instant Foods has international demand from Dubai, the UK and the US. They sell from several grocery stores across Nigeria. Kido and Kelechi are actively understanding how to scale their business to meet their demand. You can find them at http://www.dilishinstantfoods.com

However, before any of this, on the first day of our bootcamp in Lagos, Kelechi showed up with a plastic bag full of cowpeas. We asked him a bunch of questions and we learned something interesting. Kelechi was testing an assumption. Could they sell cowpeas out of a plastic bag? Or would they need to pay for fancy packaging to get people to even try their product to give them feedback?

Kelechi couldn't exactly walk around with hands and pockets full of loose cow peas, he'd need to package them in something. And he hadn't yet gotten to a point where he could build factory lines, buy raw cardboard in bulk, or spend lots of money on a brand logo and colors for tens of thousands of bags of cow peas. Kelechi first needed to figure out how many beans would go into each bag, then start selling the stuff. He thought that he could do that with easy, low-cost plastic bags. That could be a perilous proposition, since he wanted his product to seem high quality from day one. Would real consumers actually buy his product if he postponed the costs of making high-quality packaging? He didn't know. This was his current riskiest assumption.

One of the most precious things for you as you seek to build your product is your time. Of all the many things you could push forward today, which is the ONE THING you're going to focus on and learn?

We've seen our entrepreneurs benefit from listing out all of their assumptions, prioritizing them along two dimensions:

- ❧ Which of these assumptions can I test now?
- ❧ What is the impact of getting this assumption wrong?

You might want to think about these assumptions through a few different categories:

- ❧ Customer behavior
- ❧ Operational requirements
- ❧ Marketing
- ❧ Organizational requirements
- ❧ Product design
- ❧ Competitor's behavior
- ❧ Supplier / raw material availability
- ❧ Third party partnerships or dependencies
- ❧ Regulatory issues / approvals

Below, we've created tables with examples from Dilish Foods, Prima Dona and Boxes and Foxes. In each row, we stated each assumption made by the founder, the impact of getting that assumption wrong, the High/Medium/Low risk factor of getting that assumption wrong and the testing plan.

Dilish Foods Riskiest Assumptions

Category	Assumption	What is the impact of being wrong?	High/ Med/ Low	Can I test it now?
Customer Behavior	If we do everything right (i.e. we get the price right, the marketing right, the operations right, etc), our consumers would want to buy pre-processed cow peas, versus ones they'd need to prepare themselves.	If we're wrong, no one will buy our product, and our business will fail.	High	No
Marketing	We should price at $2 per bag.	If we price too high, we'll sell much less than we should. If we price too low, consumers might think we're low-quality.	Med	No
Product Design	We should package cow peas in bags, not boxes. (Bags are way easier to pack, cheaper, and high-quality. Likely boxes would need bags inside, anyway, to keep the cow peas fresh.)	Getting this one wrong would mostly be a question of brand perception. If our competitors package in boxes, our product might look inferior.	Med	No

Category	Assumption	What is the impact of being wrong?	High/ Med/ Low	Can I test it now?
Customer Behavior	To test price and value prop, start out by selling in plastic bags (before we figure out our final packaging).	If consumers won't buy cow peas in plastic bags, our price and value prop experiments will fail (since consumers will be making their decision mostly on the packaging, versus on the price or the value to them).	High	Yes
3rd party relationships	Since we won't be able to produce large volumes of cow peas initially, we should start out with high-end retailers as clients.	If we seek to sell through high-end retailers first, and we can't get on their shelves, we'll waste lots of time in trying to develop business with them.	Med	No
Marketing	Once we have a product we can sell at scale, we should market primarily through radio ads.	If our target consumers don't listen much to radio ads, or if our radio ads aren't effective, we'll waste time, effort, and money, and have to start over through some other marketing channel (like Facebook, newspaper, or printed flyers at markets).	Med	No

Category	Assumption	What is the impact of being wrong?	High/ Med/ Low	Can I test it now?
Product Design	It's not worth the cost of putting informational materials (like recipes) on the back of each of our packages.	If our end-product isn't super easy for our consumers to incorporate into their day-to-day habits, we'll have to start over and figure out what should.	Low	No

Prima Dona Riskiest Assumptions

Category	Assumption	What is the impact of being wrong?	High/Med/Low	Can I test it now?
Operations	The quality of clothing made by tailors in Kenya and Nigeria will match the expectations of professionals all over the world.	If the quality is off, I need to find a new way to manufacture that is still ethical.	High. If people aren't happy with the quality, our reputation is tainted.	Yes. Make a sample garment and have Ioana and three other professionals wear it for a full day and give feedback.

Category	Assumption	What is the impact of being wrong?	High/Med/Low	Can I test it now?
Customer behavior	People want statement clothing that's unique and have a story attached to it.	No one will buy	Medium. Because these are made-to-order, I will have no purchases and no business, but I will not lose money.	Yes. Do detailed sketches and samples and post them on Instagram to gauge reaction.
Marketing	People will buy clothing online from a brand they have never heard of.	No one will buy	High. If people don't buy, we have no business since we are NOT setting up a physical store.	Yes. Run an Instagram ad and point them to the website.
Operations	Tailors will be able to keep up with high demand	We'll look disorganized and customers will be unhappy with wait times	Medium.	*Set expectations with customers whose orders haven't been fulfilled, and don't charge them until they their garments have been delivered. *Find other tailors in emerging markets who can share the load

Boxes and Foxes Riskiest Assumption

Category	Assumption	What is the impact of being wrong?	High/ Medium/ Low	Can I test it now?
Marketing	Startup founders will be interested in my help.	We have no business.	High	Set up a Facebook ad to point to my website to gauge interest.
Marketing	I'll be able to come up with an attractive pricing for my services.	Founders will decide not to use my service because it's out of their price range.	Med	Adjust price in a series of tests.
Operations	I'll be able to solve their specific problem.	Will hurt my reputation and no one will recommend me to others.	High	Reaching out to 5 founders and understanding their specific problem.
Operations	I'll be able to keep up with demand.	Time-pressed founders will become frustrated with a lack of responsiveness.	Med	Clearly setting expectations with founders, turning down work and creating worksheets.

Category	Assumption	What is the impact of being wrong?	High/ Medium/ Low	Can I test it now?
Marketing	People beyond my own network will be willing to pay a stranger up front for business advice.	My business will not scale beyond people who know me personally.	Med	Ask satisfied customers to spread the word among their networks.

So let's try this with your idea.

1. In the workbook, fill in the first column of your Riskiest Assumptions. Write down every single assumption you're making for your business. There will be a lot! Don't worry too much about whether the assumption is too big or too small. Right now, all you want to do is get it down on the page.

2. Next, we want to go through each assumption and think about the impact to our business if we get it wrong. In your workbook, in the second column, describe what the impact might be.

3. In the third column, let's classify whether the potential impact of getting it wrong is High, Medium, or Low.

4. In the fourth column, let's figure out if you can test your assumption today and how.

Test Your Riskiest Assumption

Remember Dr. Moses, the young Nigerian doctor saving women and babies from maternal mortality?

His riskiest assumption was this: that women would come to be tested if he offered mobile ultrasounds in their villages. He knew that these tests would save lives. He knew he could get the equipment. He knew his price was about right. But… would people in rural areas overcome societal norms and accept modern medicine?

Previously, for his clinic he'd bought an old bulky machine that wasn't portable. He and his assistant had driven to villages, picked up patients and transported them back to his clinic to run the sonograms. That previous method was slow — they could only see about four patients daily. Dr. Moses had a theory that if he could take mobile ultrasounds TO the villages, he could run many more sonograms by cutting down the time and cost of commuting. Plus, he could also see patients who weren't able to travel.

How did Dr. Moses test his riskiest assumption? He borrowed a mobile ultrasound machine from a hospital that had the equipment but couldn't use it — they had no Sonologist (turns out to be a pretty scarce skill in Nigeria). Dr. Moses and his assistant drove to four villages and offered sonograms at the local community center.

Word about this life-saving technology spread quickly through the villages. Dr. Moses had women lining up for sonograms in all four of the remote villages — Doma and Lafia in Nassarawa, Adoka in Benue and Anyama Ijaw in Bayelsa. Dr. Moses, therefore, answered "yes" to both his questions: Would they come? Yes. Would they accept modern medicine? YES.

During his tests, Dr. Moses also discovered he could conduct four mobile ultrasounds an hour, versus his previous four mobile ultrasounds a DAY. The saving on time from not having to physically drive women to his clinic, was immense.

Unfortunately, he had to return the borrowed ultrasound machine once the hospital found a Sonologist, but by then he had realized that he needed to purchase one of his own. His business had real potential.

Prima Dona Example

For Prima Dona, the two riskiest assumptions were that:

- ❧ The quality of clothing made by tailors in emerging markets would match the expectations of professionals all over the world
- ❧ People would buy clothing online from a brand they have never heard of

This is how Dona tested them:

1. She drew a detailed sketch with a wrap dress design, complete with photos of the exact fabric she would use. She shared the design on Instagram, and 10 people she did not know responded positively with "I want that"
2. She ordered a test wrap-dress with the fabric she'd chosen, working with Leah and a tailor in Kenya. Dona then asked three unbiased acquaintances to try on the test garment. All three wanted to keep it. Ioana won!
3. Her next step will be to use the same design, order new individual dresses for these acquaintances, and sell to them. She will accept payment via a simple payment mechanism such as cash in person, PayPal or writing a check, before she takes the time to set up a website.

Boxes and Foxes Example

For Boxes and Foxes, the two riskiest assumptions were that:

- Startup founders will be interested in Jeremiah's help
- He'll be able to help them with their specific problem

This is how Jeremiah tested them:

1. Jeremiah reached out to five startup founders he knew (who weren't part of the fellowship) to ask them each of them for a specific problem they were struggling with in their business.
2. For each of their problems, he created a worksheet to address their specific challenge, and scheduled time with each one to walk them through the process. Their first five challenges were on things like their operations, business model and price.
3. As we're publishing this book, he's continuing to work with these initial five on new challenges they encounter, as well as helping new founders who find Boxes and Foxes at his website (www.boxesandfoxes.com) — keep checking in to learn what happens! (If you're interested yourself, you can also reach out!)

Starting a business is all about prioritizing the investment of your time, energy, people, and funds. Before you start, there's very little that you know. Nearly everything is risky, so it's critical that you prioritize. Looking back at the previous section where you listed your assumptions, what are the ABSOLUTE BIGGEST things you don't know and need to test?

You should test your riskiest assumptions WITH your hero
and people like them with similar buying characteristics
and WITHOUT spending a lot of money or time.

We highly recommend that you DO NOT TEST on friends or family as they will definitely bias your demand expectations.

Doing this will help you understand whether your idea might be a solution — in which case you should move on to testing the NEXT set of riskiest assumptions — or NOT, which can help you decide if you need to move onto another idea.

In your workbook, write down:

What are the riskiest assumptions you have?

How will you test these with the lowest cost test possible?

Begin to Craft Your Solution

He walked up the six flights of stairs to the Co-Creation Hub in Yaba, a big smile on his face despite the nervousness in his heart. He was determined to help ensure that others don't go through what his father had, several months prior. His name is Bem Asen and he is an elder advocate. Bem was one of the Nigerian fellows whose origin story moved us deeply.

Bem's 56-year-old father had held down a job with the Nigerian government for 25 years. One day, however, he was suddenly let go. He started looking for jobs everywhere, but no one called him back. Bem tried to help his dad submit his resume, but quickly realized that his father's skills and decades of experience did not stand out among the thousands of others applying for the same jobs.

Bem sought advice from people in his community. That's when he quickly realized there was a far bigger problem — many veterans and older citizens in Nigeria who retire from their government and military jobs after decades of service fall into poverty without government pensions. Unemployed, many fall sick and depend entirely on the meager earnings of their families. Their plight lessens national productivity and causes many social issues.

Like many people who live in Nigeria's Benue State, Bem had pursued a future in agriculture. At the University of Ilorin, he studied zoology and parasitology. Yet for his father and so many others like him, Bem realized he needed to solve *this* problem. He founded Retire Forward, an online platform connecting retired workers and veterans to organizations offering training, jobs, internships, loans, business grants and many other opportunities. His platform would be the first of its kind in Nigeria.

They planned to work both online and offline to connect this older demographic group to credible organizations willing to give them a chance to reinvest their experience into the economy. They'd teach them new skills to meet 21st century needs.

We were profoundly struck by Bem's story. It's a global problem. It's affecting our own parents now... and will definitely affect us in the future. Even in Silicon Valley, ageism is a real problem. We knew that if Bem could solve this problem in Nigeria, his solution might be able to scale to the entire world.

By this point, Bem had already performed thorough tests for several of his Riskiest Assumptions. One was that organizations would be willing to fill part-time roles with retired workers. He'd gone out and talked to lots of companies that told him that, if the situation was right, they'd consider hiring retirees. Another Riskiest Assumption he'd tested was that he could find retired people qualified to fill those roles. Using the jobs from the companies he'd talked to as a base, he was able to identify retirees who would be able to win those jobs, and willing to try them out if they weren't too far from home and if they paid enough. His next Riskiest Assumption was that he could make money from such a practice.

Bem was now at the stage where he needed to set up a working prototype to test this Assumption. It was well and good to conduct surveys and interviews. But to be able to collect real money from organizations whose jobs he'd filled with retirees, he needed a prototype. Bem needed to build a Minimum Viable Product (MVP).

In his case, he needed to find the easiest (and cheapest) way to connect organizations with people.

His initial idea was to set up a website matching elders with establishments that needed part-time help. Bem described his plans to hire a team to build a website with profile pages and a matching algorithm.

Tunji Eloso, one of the co-founders of CCHub and the Director of Pre-Incubation there, is a prototype master. We learned a great deal by merely listening to Tunji simplify our fellows' prototypes to fit the needs of the local market. When he heard Bem's plan to make a matching website, he shook his head violently. Such a site would be expensive and time-consuming to keep live and current, especially since Bem wasn't a software engineer.

"NO NO NO. No, you don't need a website. You need to start with the demand side. Go to hospitals and banks. Propose to help them find a receptionist or a guard part-time. Only once they agree, do you then have demand to find an elder person to fill the role. At first, fill that role by yourself, over the phone or in person if necessary."

Tunji kept repeating this phrase:

In a minimum viable product, your customers decide what's viable (by what they'll pay for). But YOU decide what's minimum.

After listening to Tunji's advice, Bem came up with several ideas that could work. Ultimately, he decided to gather his retirees into a WhatsApp group. Whenever he had a job opportunity, he sent a message to the group. Once someone was interested, he called offices with the information to connect them.

Once Bem tested the idea and was able to create jobs for more than 60 people, he then set up a website where retirees could submit their resumes. You can find Retire Forward at: http://retireforward.org/about-us/

So, now you have a hero. You've tested your idea on your hero and other people like them. You've seen signs that your idea works. It's time to build something that's closer to what your product will actually be. How are you going to do that?

Remember, your product at this stage does NOT need to be your "forever product." You're simply testing the main interactions between the parts of your business in your solution sketch. It's your Minimum Viable Product for the current stage of your business, to test the things you need to focus on.

Model 47 (this book): Even for us while writing this book, we didn't sit down and start writing one day. Our book began its life as a dozen lessons on paper. We tested them on our 25 Nigerian entrepreneurs. Over time, we added more lessons. Some lessons split into two, three, or five. Others didn't work quite as well as we needed them to, so we evolved them or removed them altogether. We tested deeper content with our East African fellows, and other entrepreneurs we met around the world. Then we tested that content with a few other businesses our friends were starting. We tested this content 46 times with varying stages of prototype before starting to write this book. So, how can you test yours? Think bare-bones.

Kelechi/Kido of Dilish Foods (powdered cowpeas to make meal preparation easier): Their first prototype was plastic bags of handmilled cowpeas. For their second prototype, they put the cowpeas into cardboard packaging with printed words. When they noticed that the second round disintegrated when wet, they tried a third round of packaging.

Dr. Moses of Sonocare (mobile ultrasounds for rural Nigerian women): His first prototype was driving women to ultrasounds. His second prototype was borrowing a mobile ultrasound machine for a short time, to see if women would come to be tested. His third prototype was getting his own machine. He is now scaling to get more machines and an assistant. His customers do not have smartphones or computers so he has to physically show up to a village and spread the word.

Leah of Mshonaji (matching tailors with people who want unique fashion): For her first prototype, she used Facebook messenger and WhatsApp for her transactions with customers and the tailors. Once she has a large number of customers, she can build a website to directly connect tailors and customers.

Omasiri of Chart Synergy (digitized medical records): His first prototype was a website with a form to fill in patient info. Because the hospital had computers, he was able to do this. If they didn't, he'd need a different solution – like making a smartphone or feature phone app. His second prototype was a database to store the information and a more sophisticated input form.

Yinka of Lawcademy (online law education platform)– For his first prototype, Yinka wrote down lessons he'd created previously, and verbal lessons he did in person with a focus group. He video recorded himself giving these lessons as his second prototype, and distributed these on USB memory stick keys. For his third prototype, he put his lessons up on a website.

Damiola of Greenpad Concepts (biodegradable, locally made sanitary pads for women) – For his first prototype, Damiola made pads from banana fiber and handed them out in person. For his second, he got help from others to assemble packs of pads. His third prototype will use a machine to make pads from banana fiber.

Dona for Prima Dona (ethically made statement people) – drew sketches with examples of real designs and fabric and shared them on Instagram to see the reaction from people she does not know. She also shared real pictures of her test garments to gauge reactions and ran an Instagram ad pointing to her website.

Jeremiah for Boxes and Foxes (business advice for non-traditional founders) – made a website with a detailed submission form so entrepreneurs could share with him the types of business challenges troubling them. He then reached out to his network, encouraging them to point their founder friends to the form. He worked with each of the interested founders through email, WhatsApp and text messaging to start each of them off with a worksheet to deeply understand their business challenge. He then followed up with a phone call with each founder to discuss potential solutions.

Now it's your turn to fill out the workbook. What is a low-cost way to build your product?

Co-Create with Your Hero

Damilola Samuel had a problem. He could not truly test his product… because he didn't have the necessary body parts himself.

If you recall from earlier, Damilola is an agripreneur making sanitary pads so rural girls can attend school during their menstrual cycles. When Damilola made his first prototype of banana fiber sanitary pads (that biodegrade MUCH faster than western world made pads), villagers were skeptical. "I first started visiting schools to share the concept, but of course the teachers said, 'You're a man. What do you know about women's issues?'" Damilola says. "But after two women joined my team, the teachers were welcoming and open to talking about our product. (The two are now Chief Operating Officer and Program Coordinator.)"

But this was not enough. Damilola knew he had to test his product with his target audience: rural girls. He gave free pads to 30 school girls at Idanre High School and 70 girls at Anglican Grammar School, both in southwest Nigeria. The girls gleefully embraced the sanitary pads and the information Damilola's team provided. The girls also gave them feedback on both the product and the packaging. One of the girls told him that, before reading his information, she'd had no idea how unsafe it was to use tissue paper, notebook paper and other material to take care of herself during her period.

His colleagues pushed Damilola to do even more to involve women in the process. The team began to hire rural women for their product development, weaving banana and plantain stems into the fiber needed for the pads. Today, seven women farmers make and help distribute Greenpads.

Omasiri, CEO of Chart Synergy, was eager to do even more to digitize hospital patient records. "I've really wanted to build artificial intelligence (AI) into our solution," he told us. "Our bigger vision is to use data and AI to help doctors make better decisions. But right now, we're focusing on the basics."

Although Omasiri had initially built AI features into Chart Synergy, while marketing the solution he quickly discovered that many Nigerian hospitals first needed to gain comfort with technology — the internet and computers. They weren't yet ready to see the benefits of AI, let alone incorporate it into their operations. It's a lesson that most entrepreneurs have encountered when developing a minimum viable product – the right question isn't necessarily "Can this product be built?" but rather "Should this product be built?"

Omasiri refocused his product on addressing customers' core needs at a deeper level. His team built an affordable digital-records solution that didn't require costly servers, special hardware, or even constant connectivity to the internet. Now that Chart Synergy serves multiple clients, the positive impact they report can help the company reach even more customers. As demand grows, then the team can evaluate adding additional features to the product.

We're big believers in co-creating. Back in the 90s, it was enough to have transactional relationships. The company sold a product to a customer. The customer handed the company money. Everyone went home. The company didn't care if the customer liked the product, used it, would use it a second or a third time, or would recommend it.

> Co-creation is no longer optional. These days, the initial purchase
> is just the beginning of the relationship — not its end.

Remember the hero you identified earlier in the book? You must co-create with them to make sure that your solution actually solves their problem. After all, how else can you make sure that you are in fact, solving the problem? How can you work to ensure your hero will use your product again AND recommend it to people like them?

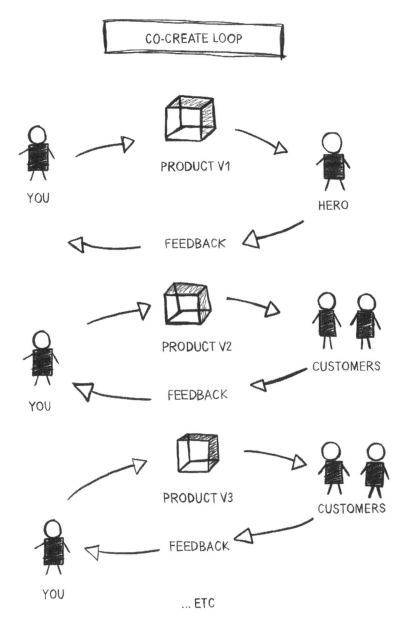

Prima Dona Example

For Prima Dona, Dona has identified a group of five people to share her sketches and fabric options with via a WhatsApp group. Once people weigh in on their favorites, she has the garment made by tailors that Leah finds. Her customers are immediately inclined to buy these garments since they had a hand in the creating them.

One change she made as a result of feedback from her customers was adding extra buttons for more coverage in a professional setting. This was for the first wrap dress she designed.

Boxes and Foxes Example

For Boxes and Foxes, Jeremiah creates custom worksheets for each founder. To do this, he first starts with the worksheets that he's used for previous business challenges as well as the feedback he's received for each one. He then tailors offerings on his website to match these frameworks. He then asks the founders to spread the word among their networks.

One change he made as a result of feedback was around the break-even worksheet. Several founders told him the model he was using was too complex for someone without an advanced degree. He simplified it to the bare-bones for someone solving a real start-up problem rather than trying to pass a business school course.

A second change he made was introducing the idea of a phone call to talk through the challenge. Previously he'd only had a series of tailored worksheets, but founders told him they needed an unbiased, knowledgeable person to talk through their problem and potential solution.

How are you providing your product to the hero you identified earlier?

How are you taking in their feedback?

What changes are you making as a result of their feedback?

Understand Your Goals

By now you should have a pretty good idea of what your business is, who it will serve and what the solution will look like. Now it's time to think about timelines and goals. This is what we call the Dreaming Big portion of the program. We're firm believers that when you write down a dream, it becomes a goal and you can start to work toward it. Often this exercise will help you think bigger and more ambitiously. This is GREAT information for you to have as you build your team or figure out how to tell your story.

This exercise sounds kind of new-agey, but it really does work. Write down the answers if your workbook. Dream BIG. Trust us!

- **What is today's date?**
- **What is the date a year from today?**
- **What is a dream you have for your business for one year from now? Just write everything that comes to your head. Totally free form and in the present tense. *(Write down the dream like this, "The year is 2020 and my business has 1000 customers who have purchased my product....")***
- **What is the date five years from today?**
- **What is a dream you have for your business five years from today? Just write everything that comes to your head. Totally free form and in the present tense.**
- **What is the date fifteen years from today?**
- **What is a dream you have for your business fifteen years from today? Just write everything that comes to your head. Totally free form and in the present tense.**

Now, the practical part.

- ☙ **What are five things you need to do THIS YEAR to make your one-year dream happen? (set up a website, get 1000 customers, make some amount of money, etc)**
- ☙ **What are five things you need to do in the next 3 MONTHS to make your one-year dream happen?**
- ☙ **What are five things you need to do THIS MONTH to make your one-year dream happen?**

Prima Dona Example

The dreaming part.

- ☙ **What is today's date?** *12/12/2018*
- ☙ **What is the date a year from today?** *12/12/2019*
- ☙ **What is a dream you have for your business for one year from now? Just write everything that comes to your head. Totally free form and in the present tense.**

  The year is 2019 and my business, Prima Dona has 100 satisfied customers who have ordered pieces more than once. These 100 customers are showcased on the website. The tailors I have worked with are making a living wage.

- ☙ **What is the date five years from today?** *12/12/2023*
- ☙ **What is a dream you have for your business five years from today? Just write everything that comes to your head. Totally free form and in the present tense.**

  The year is 2023 and my business Prima Dona has thousands of satisfied customers, many of them showcased on the website. These customers have become friends with each other and often point out interesting opportunities to each other.

  I'm very excited to announce that we have opened our first physical store in Seattle where we sell both men's and womenswear, everything still designed in Seattle and tailored in emerging markets.

The tailors I work with now manage teams of tailors and are able to scale to do the work.

ଔ **What is the date fifteen years from today?** *12/12/2033*

ଔ **What is a dream you have for your business fifteen years from today? Just write everything that comes to your head. Totally free form and in the present tense.**

The year is 2033 and my business Prima Dona has millions of satisfied customers, many of them showcased on the website. Fast fashion is dead and people enjoy buying and having clothing for years and decades rather than a season.

The tailors I have worked with for years now have their own thriving tailoring businesses in emerging markets all over the world.

We have Prima Dona stores all over the world, including in Seattle, New York, Austin, Miami, London, Denmark, Nigeria, Kenya, Australia, Korea, Argentina and more.

Now, the practical part.

ଔ **What are five things you need to do THIS YEAR to make your one-year dream happen? (set up a website, get 1000 customers, make some amount of money, etc)**

> *Set up a website*
> *Get 100 customers*

ଔ **What are five things you need to do in the next 3 MONTHS to make your one-year dream happen?**

> *Set up a website with an ecommerce option*
> *Get 10 customers and showcase them on the website*
> *Have a pop-up so people can try on the pieces*
> *Do a social media campaign to draw attention to the website. The pictures should be happy customers with testimonials.*
> *Get a reliable set of tailors lined up to do the work.*

ଔ **What are five things you need to do THIS MONTH to make your one-year dream happen?**

> *Set up a website*
> *Test with my 3 first customers and ask them to each refer 3 people—name pieces after these first 3 customers.*

❧ *Gauge readiness of the tailors doing the work in Kenya and Nigeria*
❧ *Figure out logistics of doing a pop-up—how many pieces do I need? What size? Where will it be?*

Boxes and Foxes Example

The dreaming part.

ଔ **What is today's date?** *12/14/2018*

ଔ **What is the date a year from today?** *12/14/2019*

ଔ **What is a dream you have for your business for one year from now? Just write everything that comes to your head. Totally free form and in the present tense.**

The year is 2019 and my business, Boxes and Foxes has helped unblock 50 startup founders on their businesses. We have covered topics ranging from finance to customer engagement to social media.

ଔ **What is the date five years from today?** *12/14/2023*

ଔ **What is a dream you have for your business five years from today? Just write everything that comes to your head. Totally free form and in the present tense.**

The year is 2023 and my business Boxes and Foxes has helped 1,000 startup founders unblock their businesses. I have conducted office hours in 20 cities all over the word

ଔ **What is the date fifteen years from today?** *12/12/2033*

ଔ **What is a dream you have for your business fifteen years from today? Just write everything that comes to your head. Totally free form and in the present tense.**

The year is 2033 and my business Boxes and Foxes has helped unblock millions of founders. I'm called on to speak at conferences all over the world and I am able to choose founders who are solving long-standing social issues to help 1:1.

Now, the practical part.

- **What are five things you need to do THIS YEAR to make your one-year dream happen? (set up a website, get 1000 customers, make some amount of money, etc)**
    - Finish M47
    - Finish my website
    - Get 50 customers
- **What are five things you need to do in the next 3 MONTHS to make your one-year dream happen?**
    - Finish my website, and make sure it has an ecommerce option
    - Get 10 customers and unblock their business problems
    - On my website and in my marketing, tell the stories of these 10 customers
- **What are five things you need to do THIS MONTH to make your one-year dream happen?**
    - Finish my website, and if e-commerce is too difficult
    - Test with my 3 first customers: Rachel, Ioana and Andres

The Tools of Act 1

Have you been filling out your workbook?

If so, you should have about one page for each of these tools:

- ೞ What is the overview of your idea? (We call this our "Sh#tty First Draft.)
- ೞ Your "Why Me" Statement
- ೞ Who Is Your Hero? (Build for One)
- ೞ Problem Definition
- ೞ Solution Sketch
- ೞ Alternatives (Competition) and Differentiators
- ೞ Segmentation (Finding the Gowons)
- ೞ Target Audience(s)
- ೞ Positioning
- ೞ Value Proposition
- ೞ List of Riskiest Assumptions
- ೞ Riskiest Assumption Test (RAT)
- ೞ Minimum Viable Product (MVP)
- ೞ Co-Create Loop
- ೞ Your Near and Future Goals

ACT II

Do You Have a Hobby, a Business or a Non-Profit?

There are a LOT of coffee meetings in the entrepreneurial world. It feels like the best conversations and deals take place over cups of coffee. So, the two of us started thinking. In addition to this book, what if we could create a place where entrepreneurs could gather, drink coffee, work, network and host events. We are exploring the idea of opening such a space in Seattle called Origin Stories Coffee as part of our Origin Stories business. After all, every hero has an Origin Story and we'd love to foster a physical meeting of these heroes.

To help us think through whether Origin Stories Coffee will be a hobby, a business or a non-profit, we completed the next section and showcased this business as the primary example.

It's your turn to do the same. Now, that you've established that your idea is a good one, and that you' will, in fact, have some customers, it's time to answer the next important question: do you have a hobby, a business or a non-profit?

Dona finds this section to be particularly difficult. She didn't go to business school. Although she understands that the economics are important, her superpowers are the technology, the customers and the storytelling aspects of Model 47. That said, she used this next section to figure out the numbers for Origin Stories Coffee. While it was time-consuming and difficult, she calculated the *break-even*. So will you.

Do you have a hobby, a business or a non-profit in your idea? Do Dona and Jeremiah with Origin Stories Coffee? You'll have to read to the end to find out!

Just like last time, we're first going to show you the final product; the one-page of info you'll need to know for your business. Don't be alarmed if you have no clue yet what these words and equations mean. Dona made Jeremiah use words that real people having every day conversations would use. It will all make sense by the end of Act II, we promise. (And if it doesn't, you can always write to us with your questions!)

On the next page, you'll see the one-pager for "Doing the Math." In the workbook that goes with this book, you can find a blank one to fill out. If you don't have the workbook, please copy the one-pager exactly as is into your journal.

Be ready to fill it out as you read the next few sections.

Ready? Let's go!

#DoTheMath One-Pager

You may have no idea what any of these terms mean. *DO NOT PANIC! All of these will be defined in the next few chapters.)*

[A] **Your Unit of Sale** = _____ (the thing you sell — usually the thing that shows up on the receipts you hand your customer. Sometimes more complicated, but we'll go through this in detail.)

[B] **Your Monthly Fixed Costs** = _____ (the costs you pay monthly, even if you don't actually sell anything)

[C] **Your Investment Fixed Costs** = _____ (the costs you incur before you begin, which you want to pay off at some point)

[D] **Your Costs per Unit of Sale** = _____ (the "variable" costs you pay to produce each unit, a.k.a. the "cost per goods sold" or COGS — don't worry, we'll explain this as well.)

[E] **Your Average Revenue per Unit of Sale** = _____ (this is usually, but not always, your price)

[F] **Profit per Unit** = Average revenue – Cost per Unit

_____ = [value of E] _____ - [value of D] _____

[G] **Monthly Break Even** = Monthly fixed costs / Profit per Unit

_____ = [value of B] _____ / [value of F] _____

Each month (on average), you'll need to sell **‹Monthly Break Even›** number of **‹Units of Sale›** to have a business rather than a hobby.

Know What You're Selling
(and how Customers Want to Pay for it)

As you've probably noticed, the first thing in the one-pager you need to figure out is unit of sale. It's a fancy business school term, but what does it mean? Very simply put: it's the thing you're going to charge your customers for.

Unit of Sale == what you're going to charge customers for. What is that for you? A product? A service? An hour of your time?

There are many ways to charge! A unit of sale should align with customer value and customer understanding. Many products give multiple options. (For example, a software company makes money from licenses, subscriptions, advertising, etc).

Have a look at your business sketch and figure out some things you can charge for. Sometimes it's a product. It could also be a service to help people use the product. It can be a subscription to keep that product up-to-date. You may need a few tries to figure out your initial unit of sale. That's okay! Remember, co-create with your customer. Figure out what else they're willing to pay for.

Let's look at some examples from our fellows (and also from our own businesses: Origin Stories Coffee, Dona's fashion line, Prima Dona, and Jeremiah's startup consulting, Boxes & Foxes) to help you figure out your own Unit of Sale.

Value Prop	Possible Units of Sale
For Nigerian farmers, Basmalah Enterprises pumps water less expensively than petrol-consuming generators, by using mobile solar power.	○ Per field irrigated ○ Per hectare of land pumped ○ Per gallons pumped ○ Per days pumped ○ Per half-day's pumped ○ Per hours pumped
For healthcare providers, Chart Synergy makes electronic healthcare record-keeping better and cheaper than competing platforms by providing a high-quality system for patient data collection, storage, analysis and transmission.	○ Per "seat" (per person using the Chart Synergy app) ○ Per monthly subscription to the service ○ Per patient record stored in the system ○ Installation fee ○ Maintenance fee
For pregnant women, SonoCare offers more convenient, affordable, and accurate testing than expensive, remote, understaffed, under-equipped clinics with mobile diagnostic medical imaging services.	○ Per test (EKG / Sonogram) ○ Per visit ○ Per patient
For Kenyan and international women, Mshonaji offers high-fashion custom-made clothing with a feel-good story, via a web platform employing expert Kenyan tailors using top-quality locally woven fabrics.	○ Per hour of work ○ Per garment ○ Per customer
For Seattle-based entrepreneurs, Origin Stories Coffee offers a meeting, work and event space specifically for people who are starting and running businesses and who want to interact with similar people.	○ Per cup of coffee ○ Per event
For AND people, Prima Dona offers 'timeless statement clothing with a story' more ethically than mainstream shops and boutiques, through a made-to-order process creating jobs for emerging market tailors.	○ Per garment ○ Per customer ○ Per hour of styling services

Value Prop	Possible Units of Sale
Boxes and Foxes solves startup founders' exact problems better than online learning, startup books, and traditional consultants — by offering highly-customized consulting services recommended by people like you.	❧ Per worksheet ❧ Per hour of individual consulting

What are YOUR possible Units of Sale? Write down all the possibilities in your workbook. Don't worry, we'll refine these and pick one. Right now, just brainstorm.

Many, if not most, businesses have multiple ways they make money. For example, Chart Synergy (electronic healthcare record-keeping software) could charge each of their client hospitals and clinics a fee for installation of their service, monthly access fees, and incremental fees for any changes they request. Grocery stores have many, many products on the shelves. Hair stylists charge different prices for women and men, or for different hair lengths. GreenPad Concepts (sanitary products for rural girls) sometimes sells individual pads and other times sells packages of five or ten.

To reduce complexity and to better understand the dynamics of your business, you want to pick a Primary Unit of Sale, base your calculations off it and then add more later if it makes sense. Our fellows have told us that it's far easier for them to understand how they're doing if they pick a *single* unit of sale to model their business. They either pick one unit of sale (like "charge per one field irrigated" or "charge per patient visit"), or else they assess the unit of sale on an "average sale per customer" (sometimes referred to as a "shopping cart" or "basket") basis. For instance, a grocery store would average the receipts for each customer; its unit of sale would be the *customer visit*.

Below are some of the examples we've used so far, as well as the PRIMARY unit of sale they've selected (and why). Looking at your business, what do you think will be the best primary unit of sale to help you forecast?

Value Prop	Why?
For Nigerian farmers, Basmalah Enterprises pumps water less expensively than petrol-consuming generators, by using mobile solar power. **PRIMARY unit of sale?** Per field pumped	Basmalah Enterprises selected "per field pumped" for two reasons. First, this metric was *simplest for its customers to understand* and compare to the main alternative (the cost of pumping their fields with a petrol-powered generator). Second, *the costs of the business are driven in large part by the number of fields serviced.* Pumping water to one field will tie up a set of company resources (laborer, wheelbarrow, solar panel, battery, charge controller, wires, etc) essentially for a half day. Except for the laborer's time, all of the components of the set are already paid for (i.e. "fixed"), and the laborer can be paid "per field" as well.
For Nigerian healthcare providers, Chart Synergy makes electronic healthcare record-keeping better and cheaper than competing platforms by providing a high-quality system for patient data collection, storage, analysis and transmission. **PRIMARY unit of sale?** Per "seat," (per person using the app)	Chart Synergy selected "per seat" because this metric was *simplest for its customers to understand*, and also because their clients were wary of subscription-based pricing. Clients were looking for a pricing model that they could pay once and be done with, and not one that they'd need to worry about down the road. Since Chart Synergy is software, most of *its costs* are driven by the upfront time its software developers took to write, test, and deploy that software.

Value Prop	Why?
For pregnant women, SonoCare offers more convenient, affordable, and accurate testing than expensive, remote, understaffed, under-equipped clinics with mobile diagnostic medical imaging services. **PRIMARY unit of sale?** Per test	SonoCare selected "per test" because this metric was *simplest for its customers to understand*. The business could also model its costs by estimating the number of tests it could perform each day, week, and month.
For Seattle-based entrepreneurs, Origin Stories Coffee offers a meeting, work and event space specifically for people who are starting and running businesses and who want to interact with similar people. **PRIMARY unit of sale?** Per cup of coffee	It's simple for customers to understand and buying coffee is something many entrepreneurs do regularly as part of their daily lives.
For AND people, Prima Dona offers 'timeless statement clothing with a story' more ethically than mainstream shops and boutiques, through a made-to-order process creating jobs for emerging market tailors. **PRIMARY unit of sale?** Per garment	Prima Dona selected per garment because it's simple to calculate costs and revenue and the cost of most garments are similar.
Boxes and Foxes solves startup founders' exact problems better than online learning, startup books, and traditional consultants—by offering highly-customized consulting services recommended by people like you. **PRIMARY unit of sale?** Per business challenge	Foxes & Boxes selected per business challenge because it makes the most sense to its customers (other founders). It's simpler to predict revenue, since founders want to solve ONE business challenge, regardless of how many worksheets they fill out or hours on the phone. As Boxes and Foxes works with ever more founders, they can do a better job of estimating their costs based on the complexity of an average challenge.

From now own, whenever we refer to your Unit of Sale, we mean your Primary Unit of Sale. Good? Right then, in your workbook — where you have the one-pager from the beginning of this act — please write down your Unit of Sale both in the table like the above as well as the #DoTheMath one-pager.

Your Unit of Sale = _____
(the thing you sell — usually the thing that shows up on the receipts you hand your customer

Figure Out Your Costs

Next up is everyone's least favorite thing: the costs! Running a business is expensive. Sometimes we don't even realize how many costs we'll have until we list them all out! Making it even more complex is that there are several types of costs that will impact your business.

So, let's take it from the beginning, step-by-step. We're going to walk through the example of our coffee shop business, Origin Stories Coffee. To simplify the example, we're going to assume that we ONLY make and serve coffee at Origin Stories. Eventually, we want this to be a workspace and event location where we will also serve a bit of food and drinks at night. But for now, let's keep things simple.

You might want to do the same steps in your workbook so you can follow along in real time. It might take a few tries to figure out ALL of your costs. For some of our fellows, it took the whole week to remember things such as "paying for gas for their motorbike" as a cost.

Step 1: Listing out all your costs

List out everything you can think of that you'll have to spend money on whether it's a one-time cost or an on-going one. In any order, just get them down.

Origin Stories Coffee Costs

Cost Description				
A cool sign for outside				
Price list sign				
Rent				
Tables				
Chairs				
Espresso maker				
Mugs				
To-go cups				
Lids				
Straws				
Napkins				
Coffee beans				
Milk				
Electricity				
Water				
Insurance				
Staff salary				
Candles				
Blankets				
Sound system				
Ice				
Refrigerator				
Dishwasher				
Wi-fi				

Step 2: Figure out the Unit and Price Per Unit

You're going to figure out the unit by which you'll pay the cost. Is it per month? Is it for a pack of 100? You'll also figure out the cost per one unit. Do the same for your business in your workbook.

Origin Stories Coffee Costs

Cost Description	Unit	Cost Per Unit (USD)		
A cool sign for outside	One sign	$100		
Price list sign	One sign	25		
Rent	Per month	10,000		
Tables	Per table	500		
Chairs	Per chair	100		
Espresso maker	One machine	10,000		
Mugs	Pack of 10	50		
To-go cups	Pack of 100	20		
Lids	Pack of 100	20		
Straws	Pack of 100	20		
Napkins	Pack of 1000	20		
Coffee beans	10 lb bag	50		
Milk	Per gallon	5		
Electricity	Per month	500		
Water	Per month	500		
Insurance	Per month	500		
Staff salary	Per hour	25 per hour		
Candles	Pack of 10	50		
Blankets	Pack of 5	100		
Sound system	One item	1000		
Ice	20 lb bag	5		
Refrigerator	One item	1000		
Dishwasher	One item	1000		
Wi-fi	Per month	200		

Step 3: Figure out the categories of each cost

For this part, you will categorize each cost into one of the following:

Investment Fixed Costs (IFC) –These costs are ones that you start paying even before you start your business. They're an investment in the business you'd like to build, whether or not you're currently selling anything. Examples of these might be a course you took or tools you bought. The domain name for your website. A bunch of t-shirts with your company name and logo on them. An investment fixed cost is something you pay for, once, but don't to pay for again. You'll want to make enough money from your business to pay this back eventually, but we won't factor it into the day-to-day cost

Monthly Fixed Costs (MFC) - these are costs that you need to pay every month as long as your business is running. These are things such as office space, phone bills, paying salaried employees, etc. We're using monthly as a measure, but you can do weekly or quarterly if that makes better business sense for you. These are costs you will pay no matter if you sell lots of products or ZERO products.

Unit or Variable Costs are the third kind of cost you'll need to keep in mind. We call them Unit Costs because they vary according to how many units you sell. Business school-type people also refer to these costs as "costs of goods sold" or COGS. (If you sell no units, you would spend no unit/variable costs.) Some of the things that are included within your variable costs are:

- ‌ℭ The materials needed to produce your product
- ℭ Labor needed to produce your product
- ℭ The costs of delivering the product to your customer

We're going to categorize our costs for Origin Story in the table below. Please do the same for your own business.

Origin Stories Coffee Costs

Cost Description	Unit	Cost Per Unit (USD)	Cost Category
A cool sign for outside	One sign	$100	INV
Price list sign	One sign	25	INV
Rent	Per month	10,000	MFC
Tables	Per table	500	INV
Chairs	Per chair	100	INV
Espresso maker	One machine	10,000	INV
Mugs	Pack of 10	50	INV
To-go cups	Pack of 100	20	Unit
Lids	Pack of 100	20	Unit
Straws	Pack of 100	20	Unit
Napkins	Pack of 1000	20	Unit
Coffee beans	10 lb bag	50	Unit
Milk	Per gallon	5	Unit
Electricity	Per month	500	MFC
Water	Per month	500	MFC
Insurance	Per month	500	MFC
Staff salary	Per hour	25 per hour	MFC
Blankets	Pack of 5	100	INV
Sound system	One item	1000	INV
Refrigerator	One item	1000	INV
Dishwasher	One item	1000	INV
Wi-fi	Per month	200	MFC

Step 4: Calculate your total Investment Costs

Take all of the INV costs from the Step 3 table above and add them together to get a total. These are things you've already spent money on to start your business so we will NOT count them in our month-to-month cost calculations but you will need this later.

Origin Stories Coffee: Investment Costs

Description	Unit	Cost Per Unit	# Units	Subtotal
A cool sign for outside	One sign	$100	1	$100
Price list sign	One sign	$25	1	$25
Tables	Per table	$5,000	10	$5,000
Chairs	Per chair	$100	20	$2,000
Espresso maker	One machine	$10,000	1	$10,000
Mugs	Pack of 10	$50	4	$200
Blankets	Pack of 5	$100	4	$400
Sound system	One item	$1,000	1	$1,000
Refrigerator	One item	$1,000	1	$1,000
Dishwasher	One item	$1,000	1	$1,000
TOTAL INV				**$20,725**

Step 5: Calculate your total Monthly Fixed Costs

Take all the MFC costs from Step 3 and figure out how many units of each you need per month. For example, you only need to pay rent ONCE a month, however you need to pay your staff several times a month. What is the total cost TO YOU per month for each of these? Then figure out what is your total cost per month for everything?

Origin Stories Coffee: Monthly Fixed Costs (MFC)

Cost Description	Unit	Units per Month	Cost Per Unit (USD)	Cost Per Month (Unit x Cost)
Rent	Per month	1	10,000	10,000
Electricity	Per month	1	500	500
Water	Per month	1	500	500
Insurance	Per month	1	500	500

121

Cost Description	Unit	Units per Month	Cost Per Unit (USD)	Cost Per Month (Unit x Cost)
Staff salary	Per hour	40 (hours a week) x 4.3 (weeks a month) x 2 (employees) = 344 hours	25 per hour	8600
Wi-fi	Per month	1	200	200
TOTAL MFC				**20,300**

Step 6: Now comes the part that some people (ahem, Dona) finds confusing

You need to figure out your Cost Per Unit, e.g. how your business pays to produce ONE SINGLE UNIT OF SALE. With our same coffee shop example, we buy coffee beans in several-pound bags; gallon-jugs of milk; and big boxes of paper cups, cup covers, and napkins. However, we don't actually "spend" that money until we sell the cup of coffee (it sits on the shelf, just waiting for a customer to walk up to the counter). We need to figure out the cost FOR JUST ONE CUP OF COFFEE to calculate our variable costs. So — within our unit costs, we'd include the costs for just the few coffee beans that we'd grind for one cup of coffee, not the cost of the whole bag. The cost of just the milk that would go into the coffee cup, not the cost of the whole jug. The cost of one paper cup, one cup cover, a few napkins — not the entire box.

We start by listing out our Unit/Variable costs, along with the unit it was bought in. Then we calculate how many products that unit serves or produces.

Origin Stories Coffee: Costs per Unit

Cost Description	Unit (bought in)	Cost Per Unit (USD)	Serves/ Produces #	Costs Our Business (cost per unit/serves #)
To-go cups	Pack of 100	20	100 cups coffee	$20/100 = 0.20
Lids	Pack of 100	20	100 cups coffee	$20/100 = 0.20
Straws	Pack of 100	20	100 cups coffee	$20/100 = 0.20
Napkins	Pack of 1000	20	100 cups coffee	$20/100 = 0.20
Coffee beans	10 lb bag	50	700 cups coffee	$50/700 = 0.07
Milk	Per gallon	5	8 cups coffee	$5/8 = 0.63
TOTAL Cost per Unit of Sale				**$1.50**

So it costs our business $1.50 to make an average cup of coffee.

What about you? How much does it cost your business to make one unit to sell to customers?

Once you have all of these numbers, go back to the #DoTheMath one-pager at the beginning of this section and fill in your costs. We'll get to calculations next.

You should have these four items filled in now:

[A] Your Unit of Sale = _____

(the thing you sell — usually the thing that shows up on the receipts you hand your customer.

For Origin Stories, this is "a cup of coffee"

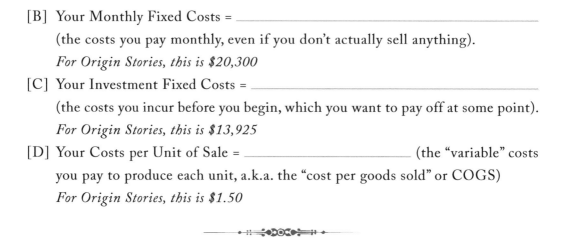

[B] Your Monthly Fixed Costs = _____

(the costs you pay monthly, even if you don't actually sell anything).

For Origin Stories, this is $20,300

[C] Your Investment Fixed Costs = _____

(the costs you incur before you begin, which you want to pay off at some point).

For Origin Stories, this is $13,925

[D] Your Costs per Unit of Sale = _____ (the "variable" costs

you pay to produce each unit, a.k.a. the "cost per goods sold" or COGS)

For Origin Stories, this is $1.50

The fourth and final costs are called Opportunity Costs. These are the benefits you *didn't receive,* because of a choice that you made or an action you took. For simplicity's sake, we don't include opportunity costs in the break-even calculation you'll use. (In some sense, the topic is too complex for that calculation.) However, for completeness we're including a short description of opportunity costs because, depending on the nature of your business, the way that you finance your business, and the timing of your revenue, understanding that this concept exists can be important.

Probably the most common form of opportunity cost is your own time. If you're starting a business instead of working at a paying job, your biggest opportunity cost is the salary *you didn't make.*

Let's assume that Suzy is a cook at a downtown restaurant in Seattle, Washington. Like most chefs, she makes minimum wage. (In Seattle, that's $15 an hour.) Most weeks she works 40 hours chopping onions, preparing sauces, and plating meals. So, each week, she makes $600, and in the average month (with 4.3 weeks) she earns $2,580. Her lifetime dream, though, has been to open a bar in Portland, Oregon. To weigh the pros and cons of actually moving to Portland and starting her business, she should properly ensure that the monthly personal profit she's making is AT LEAST $2,580. Otherwise, on a strictly financial basis, even with this amount she'd be better off NOT opening the bar in Portland and just remaining a chef. Moreover, even if Suzy gets fired from her job in Seattle, she should still "properly" include the opportunity cost in her calculations, since starting the Portland bar would (usually) REQUIRE her to give up (or "forego") the salary she *would have made*. (We told you it was complex.)

The other relevant example to consider is your financing. If you take out a loan, for example, you'll need to make monthly payments to service that loan EVERY SINGLE MONTH – even if your business is failing. ESPECIALLY if you were loaned money at a steep interest rate (anything above 5%), it might well be a better decision never to have taken that loan at all.

If you have more questions about opportunity costs, PLEASE connect with us on LinkedIn.

If you're having trouble with this, you're not alone!

> We've found that the best way to figure out your costs is to look at your sketch which should be a high-level (but good enough) reminder of the essential parts of your business.

To get a better idea how this works for a business with more fixed costs than variable costs, let's look at one of the businesses we studied earlier, Ibrahim's Basmalah solar-powered irrigation business).

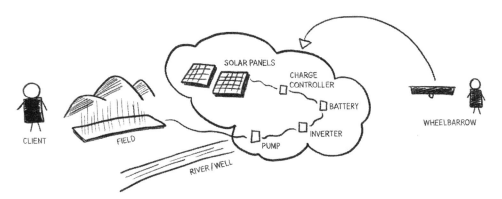

Cost Structure, Basmalah Enterprises (Solar-Powered Irrigation)

For each field that Ibrahim wants his workers to water, he needs to buy a set of equipment: two solar panels, a charge controller, a battery, an inverter, and a wheelbarrow. These are all investment fixed costs — the one-time costs: Ibrahim needs to pay these costs in advance of any sales he makes. He also needs one set of equipment for each and every field he wants to service at once — so if he wants his workers to go out and irrigate 20 fields in a single day, he needs to buy 20 sets: 40 solar panels, 20 charge controllers, etc.

Ibrahim also has several fixed monthly costs: he rents space to store his equipment, and for his sales team to make sales calls, set workers' schedules, and other administrative tasks.

In addition to these fixed costs, Ibrahim has several variable costs, which he doesn't need to pay if there's no work that day. He pays his "pumpers" (technical term for the workers who go out and actually irrigate fields) on a "per field" basis. He also allocates some miscellaneous materials (such as wire, saline for the batteries, etc) to each field they pump.

Basmalah Enterprises Cost Descriptions

Cost Categories	Cost Unit / Driver	Description
Solar Panels	Investment (buy once; use for infinite fields)	2 solar panels per field
Charge Controller	Investment	1 charge controller per field
Battery	Investment	1 battery per field
Inverter	Investment	1 inverter per field
Misc	Per field	Wires, saline, oil, etc
Wheelbarrow	Investment	1 wheelbarrow per field
"Pumper" (Direct staff)	Per field	1 "pumper" per wheelbarrow

Cost Categories	Cost Unit / Driver	Description
Indirect staff	Month	Secretary, scheduler, maintenance team, sales, etc (Ibrahim pays staff monthly)
Rent	Month	Ibrahim rents space to store his equipment, for his sales team to make sales calls, for his admin, etc

Basmalah Enterprises Costs

Potential Costs	Cost Unit / Driver	Unit Cost (each)	Number	Subtotal
Solar Panels	Investment	200,000	2	400,000
Charge Controller	Investment	80,000	1	80,000
Battery	Investment	70,000	1	70,000
Inverter	Investment	120,000	1	120,000
Misc	Every Field	10,000	1	10,000
Wheelbarrow	Investment	13,000	1	13,000
"Pumper" (Direct staff)	Every Month	35,000	7	35,000 x 7 = 245,000
Indirect staff	Every Day	500	27 staff x 30 days	27 x 500 x 30 = 405,000
Office Rent	Every Month	200,000	1	200,000

Basmalah Enterprises Investment Costs

Investment Cost Category	Nigerian Naira (N)	Quantity	Total
Solar Panels	200,000 N	14 (two per field)	2,800,000 N
Charge Controllers	80,000 N	7	560,000 N

Investment Cost Category	Nigerian Naira (N)	Quantity	Total
Batteries	70,000 N	7	490,000 N
Inverters	120,000 N	7	840,000 N
Wheelbarrows	13,000 N	7	91,000 N
		TOTAL	**4,781,000 N**

Basmalah Enterprises Monthly Fixed Costs

Monthly Cost Category	Nigerian Naira (N)	Quantity	Total
Indirect Staff (27 employees)	500 N (per person per day)	30 (days)	450,000 N
Office Rent	80,000 N	7	200,000 N
Electricity	16,000 N	1	16,000 N
Phone Bill	6,000 N	1	6,000 N
		TOTAL	**672,000 N**

Basmalah Enterprises Unit/Variable Costs

Sales Unit: Per Field

Variable Cost Category	Cost Unit	Cost per Unit (N)	Cost units per sales unit	Total
Pumper Salary	Day	500 N	1 day per field	500 N
Fabric	Bolt	10,000 N	1/10th bolt per garment	10,000 N
			TOTAL	**10,500 N**

So, for Ibrahim and Basmalah, the costs are:

[A] Your Unit of Sale = Per Field

(the thing you sell — usually the thing that shows up on the receipts you hand your customer. Sometimes more complicated, but we'll go through this in detail.)

[B] Your Monthly Fixed Costs = 672,000 N

(the costs you pay monthly, even if you don't actually sell anything).

[C] Your Investment Fixed Costs = 4,781,000 N

(the costs you incur before you begin, which you want to pay off at some point).

[D] Your Costs per Unit of Sale = 10,500 N

(the "variable" costs you pay to produce each unit, a.k.a. the "cost per goods sold" or COGS

Set A Pricing Strategy

S o, we have good news and bad news.

The bad news is that you're never going to be done setting your
final price. The good news is that this is a GOOD thing.

It's the best way to get the best value for your business during the changing seasons, the market, and expectations of customers.

For example, over the next few months both Dona and Jeremiah are going to experiment with "choose your own price" — along with higher and lower prices — to see what works better during the different seasons for their individual businesses.

Price can be a deceptively tricky part of the value equation. Entire books have been written on the subject. Usually, if you're aiming to build a "volume" business, and sell a LOT of things, you're going to want to price as low as you need to, to encourage customers to buy from you instead of from your competition. If you're seeking to build a "premium" business, you acknowledge that you'll have fewer total customers so you'll make up for this by charging a higher price. Everything is different for a few luxury goods, where a higher price actually helps drive higher volume. This is high-level intuition — but you're going to have to be more specific.

As our fellow entrepreneurs begin to set (and adapt) their prices, we've seen them have real success once they think about price in the full context of their overall business. Price is an important consideration to your consumers — as part of the comprehensive packaging / marketing of what you're selling. Taken along with everything else, your prices help consumers decide who your competitors are, what your relative quality is, how frequently and how much of your product/service they'd buy and when. Everything else equal, price is also an essential lever (maybe the MOST important lever) in how profitable your business is.

Since price is so critical to determining how well your startup does, you'll want to consider the three parts of the value equation for your business: 1) who's your hero, 2) what's your hero's problem, and 3) what would your hero be willing to pay YOU for YOUR SOLUTION to that problem? You'll use this value equation to think about your pricing strategy.

To price correctly, you absolutely need to think understand your customer very well. Remember, even for EXACTLY THE SAME PRODUCT OR SERVICE, different people will be willing to pay different prices. Good companies usually have a pricing strategy that lets them accommodate for three types of customers (call them "value-hunters," who want to pay absolutely as little as they can; "normals," who want to pay somewhere around the middle of the pack and don't want to be thought of as "cheap;" and "premiums," who actually are willing to pay more than most customers for special features or the ability to show off their status.)

Price is only ONE of the many factors that go into their decision. So you need to set your prices in the full context of all of these other factors. You need to understand not only how your hero thinks about price in relation to your product, but also what their buying behaviors are (Where do they buy? Why do they buy? How do they buy? How frequently do they buy? What are they accustomed to paying?), and what goes into their decision-making, in addition to price? (Is quality the most important thing? Bragging rights? Are they looking for something that's durable and long lasting? Or something that they'll use just once, or casually?)

Let's take a look at some pricing strategies you could consider. Let's start with the four most common "flawed" ways of pricing, each with some fairly serious shortcomings.

Flawed strategy 1: Pick a number: Randomly make up a price, and hope it works. Don't do this. Most people guess wrong. They'll pick a price that's too low and miss out on profit. Or they'll pick a price that's too high and miss out on sales from people willing to buy at a lower (but still profitable) price.

Flawed strategy 2: Cost-plus: First, pick your sales target, then figure out the average cost based on the sales target. Price is average cost plus a markup. For example, if the garment tailoring company Mshonaji used cost-plus, they might calculate that the average costs to produce a new dress is $30. The company CEO, Leah, wants to ensure that she's making a profit on each sale, so she adds a 10% markup to each sale, so offers her customers a price of $33.

Cost-plus is a weak pricing strategy for three reasons: 1) Consumers don't actually care how much a product costs to make. They want to pay "a fair price." 2) Cost-plus pricing doesn't reward minimizing costs, since the markup is dependent on costs. 3) Cost-plus pricing makes it hard to price differently for different types of consumers. Some consumers might come right to you (so they're not that expensive to find), and be extremely cost-sensitive. Since your price drives their purchase, and since it costs you less to serve these customers, you'd want to be able to offer them a *lower* price. Other, more valuable clients might care less about your price — they're driven by convenience or status, or some other factor.

Perhaps the most critical flaw in cost-plus, however, is that you have to pick the right sales target. Sell too few units, and suddenly you're *losing money* on every single unit you're selling. Cost-plus is lazy, and risky, to be quite honest. As an M47 entrepreneur with lots of hustle, you can sometimes win by lowering your prices, sometimes by raising them — so hustle and don't be lazy! #DoTheMath!

Flawed strategy 3: Pricing based only on competition: Find the alternatives to your product, and check their prices. Set your prices a little above, or a little below. Call this a "strategic" pricing strategy, and go enjoy your coffee. For example, if Mshonaji used competition-based pricing, they might calculate other tailors in Kenya are charging consumers around $33 per garment (perhaps they're using cost-plus). Leah thinks that her company offers slightly-higher quality tailoring and better service, so she sets her prices slightly higher, at $36 per garment.

But is this right? The biggest problem with this method is that it's competition-focused, not consumer-focused. What if the competition is lazy? What if they're setting prices with cost-plus or "make it up?" They're just as human as you are. We're not saying you shouldn't look at what the competition is pricing. However, we're pointing out that you shouldn't *only* look at the competition in setting your prices. You should use other information as well.

Flawed strategy 4: Negotiation pricing: Charge different prices to different consumers. Increase (or decrease) your price depending on what your consumer is willing to pay. If Mshonaji used consumer-based pricing, their CEO Leah might negotiate a different price with every single consumer — for example, a lower price to a Kenyan client than a US-based client.

There's one big downside to this method: it discriminates. It penalizes people who aren't good negotiators. Too, certain groups of people (like minorities and women) tend to pay more for the exact same product. Assuming you're not selling in a market, or some other place where negotiation is the norm, there is another way.

Good business is a repeated game. You want to build your reputation and your relationships; you want your customers to buy from you again. Negotiation can drive your best customers towards a 'simpler' model, where they don't feel taken advantage of; this model encourages clients to negotiate (because they "have to,") where they ordinarily would not. If your the price depends on how much customers like your product, they'll tend to hide their interest, as well as information you could use to make your products better. They'll also be more likely to shop around to try to get "the best deal."

There has to be a better way! Here are a few pricing strategies you *should* try.

Price As Low As You Can (Profitably) Go: Consider keeping your costs as low as possible. Except for a few luxury goods (like diamond rings, premium handbags, and high-end sports cars), the lower your price is, the more sales volume you'll tend to have. Lower prices can create energy and momentum, or help reach an audience with less disposable income but attractive for other reasons: They might be the "cool kids," more loyal, more aligned with your brand; more willing to pay for other products or services. Sales can be self-reinforcing, as satisfied customers offer word-of-mouth advertising. High sales can encourage new distributors to stock your product. Keeping prices low can also deter potential competitors, who may not be able to make money at that level.

However, having a low-cost pricing strategy can be tricky. First, it's essential to develop a value prop that resonates with your target consumer over and beyond "low cost." Once you start selling at a given price, it's very difficult to *raise* that price later. Also, by keeping prices low, you train your customers to expect that price for a certain quality. An exception is if a competitor then offers an equivalent product at lower cost, or better service or quality at the same price, it can be hard to respond effectively.

One of the reasons it's so important to have an idea of what your costs are, both variable and fixed, is that this information helps you understand how low you can go on price. This is why knowing your break-even is so important. In most cases, you can't price your products for less than it costs to make them. If your variable cost to produce one unit of sale is $1.00 and your price is $.99, you're losing a penny on every sale you make. You can't make any money in the long term unless you charge at least a bit more than $1.00. Your variable cost for each product ends up becoming your "floor."

There are, of course, some exceptions. If you make money elsewhere in your business, you can sometimes use one product as your "loss leader." For example, a company like Amazon, which makes most of its revenue by selling items through its store, could afford to price some hardware products (like the Kindle) at a price lower than it costs to produce that hardware. Amazon would then seek to recoup these costs through sales of other items, such as eBooks. Another example would be a grocery story that prices milk, eggs, or some other widely-used product very low. However, this grocery store would try to recover the losses from that item through other — incremental sales — of other products the consumer would buy while in the store. Sometimes companies will also seek to try and sell products at a price that is artificially too low as an "introductory" offer (essentially marketing) to help consumers try a new product for the first time. However, over the long term, no company can stay in business by pricing its products below the variable cost to produce them, without making up for those losses in some other way.

Price slightly below (or sometimes above) competition, but at a break-even that makes sense: This pricing strategy is similar to flawed strategy #3, but incorporates an important factor: the cost structure of your own business.

Multi-sided market (including freemium and ad-based): This pricing strategy is like "low-cost," but has a key distinction: it breaks the set of consumers into at least two groups. The first group of consumers pays a little bit or nothing for some type of service (usually basic). The other group pays more for another type of service (usually fancier, or with special features). One notable example of freemium is a newspaper (which traditionally charged very low costs or nothing to their readers, but charged companies to advertise within their pages). Similar is a radio station, search engine, or website that offers "free" content to its audience, but also serves up ads. Another type of multi-sided model would be Ladies' Night at a bar, which charges men an entrance fee but lets women in for free. Typically, these sorts of models work in a "multiple-sided market," i.e. men tend to be more interested in going to a bar if they have the chance to meet women there; advertisers are more likely to pay a fee to have their ad appear alongside content if they know that their own desired consumers are likely to be consuming that content.

Reinvent the Value Exchange: Another way to price is to be flexible in your unit of sale versus competition.

One set of examples are *big-sizing campaigns* from food companies like McDonald's (e.g. large "Supersized" portions), 7-Eleven (e.g. gigantic "Big Gulp" cups), and Starbucks (e.g. "Venti"-sized coffee servings), which offer progressively larger food and beverage portion sizes at slightly higher prices. Since most restaurants are driven mostly by "fixed" costs (such as rent, electricity, and marketing) — not by "variable" costs (such as the ingredients for the food and beverage sold) — companies earn more profit from slightly higher prices for slightly bigger sizes.

"Bottom of the Pyramid"-style pricing takes the opposite approach, and offers progressively smaller portion sizes. Being able to purchase smaller units — such as sachets of laundry detergent; single-use portions of salt, sugar, butter; short-term stays at AirBnB and Uber rides — can open up the market for less-committed (or

more cost-aware) consumers. Someone who can't afford the larger size, but wants to try your product with slightly less commitment might be interested

Yet a third opportunity is just to *reframe the unit of sale.* Examples include advertising magazine subscriptions at "cost per issue" versus "cost per year." The overall price for twelve issues per year is *exactly the same as before,* but framing the costs in this way help consumers compare to other purchases (such as the price of a latte, or the price of a sandwich at lunch). Other examples are selling digital music by the song (versus by the 12-song album).

Subscriptions – Often, your best customers are repeat customers. Repeat customers can be less price sensitive, and cost less to retain. They're also great for recurring revenue (money coming in regularly). Especially if your business has multiple products or service categories, it can be in your best interest to pay attention to the specific types of products that your highest-value customers purchase. Even if those specific products don't offer you the highest of margins, if they keep your high-value customers happy, they can be worth it. In general, we want to prioritize profitable customers (not just customers that bring in lots of revenue).

The Allure of Luxe – On the other end from low-cost is luxury pricing, based on exclusivity, high quality, status, and personalized service. Your customers feel they're gaining social status, a feeling of belonging, or simply a psychological boost. Maybe you're selling a product your customers can feel proud to give as an expensive gift. Charging high prices in some cases can help attract the "right" sort of customers and suggest high value to them. This requires you to create and sustain an allure to your product and company. The strategy also requires from you the discipline to avoid discounting — the more you reduce your price, even temporarily, the harder it is to charge luxury prices in the long term.

Pay if it Works – Some products (such as certain types of software) might be great deals for your customers but seem risky up-front. A customer might not know — before trying your product — whether it will work for them. For example, Nigerian electronic record software Chart Synergy estimates its software can reduce the costs of record-keeping by half. However, some potential clients doubted they'd see results. They're concerned they'd pay a large fee for Chart Synergy software but find too late that the solution won't work for them.

For products such as this one, a "performance-based" pricing strategy help. There are two main ways to do this. One way is that the buyer pays you up front (but you offer a full refund IF certain conditions aren't met). Or, the seller only pays you AT THE END of some period of time, after meeting certain conditions.

Either way, this sort of structure encourages trial. If the seller is confident that the product will meet these conditions, using a performance-based pricing strategy can dramatically increase the number of customers who will try (and pay for) your product. This sort of strategy greatly reduces the risks for buyers concerned that an unknown or un-tested product — especially an expensive one — might fail and be a waste of their money and time.

A performance-based pricing strategy works in diverse industries. For example, the advertising industry has shifted from the traditional pay per thousand views (CPM) model to a pay per click (CPC) model, which is more of a performance-based contract. US personal-injury lawyers take ONLY one-third of SUCCESSFUL settlements, versus the hourly-fee structure common in other parts of the law, like bankruptcy. Literary agents typically take 15%. (We have a great one, by the way — Hi Elaine!) For the properties they help sell, US real estate agents tend to take 6% of the closing price. Some business or strategy consultants are trying out the strategy.

In a way, this pricing strategy also transforms the relationship between the buyer and seller from a contest (where the buyer "wins" from a lower price and the seller "wins" with a higher price) into something like a partnership (where the incentives for both are aligned behind the same goal). If done right, the buyer/seller interaction can develop into a strong, repeated relationship. For example, home buyers who stay in the same area and had a good experience with their real estate agent, tend to come back to the same agent if they decide to look for a new home.

"Pay What You Wish" – You don't have any set prices. Encourage your customer to pay what they feel is correct for them. Your customer never feels like they've overpaid — since they're responsible for setting the price. This can also be a great "marketing gimmick," as well, earning you some free word-of-mouth or maybe written advertising. If you have several products, having "pay as you wish" pricing for one of them can also drive sales of your other products. In general, these sorts of programs work best if you're selling something 1) with low variable costs (such as software or music), 2) in a marketplace with lots of aggressive competition, 3) that could be sold realistically at a broad range of prices (such as music, art, food), 4) to a set of consumers who want to be "fair," and 5) sets up or is based upon a positive relationship between the consumer and your company. This is a bit of a "new age" strategy, which won't work for most companies, but it's an interesting way to do an experiment to see what people are willing to pay. We include it for completeness, since a number of firms have found success with this strategy (Dona is using this as one of her pricing experiments to understand how much to charge her target audience).

Value Prop:

For Nigerian farmers, Basmalah Enterprises pumps water less expensively than petrol-consuming generators, by using mobile solar power.

PRIMARY Unit of Sale?

Per field pumped

Pricing Strategy:

Price slightly below competition, but at a break-even that makes sense

Why?

To pick his pricing strategy, Ibrahaim of Basmalah calculated that clients (farmers in the rural North of Nigeria) would typically pay about $70 to irrigate their fields with petrol-powered pumps. He calculated his breakeven at $70, and then looked at a variety of prices slightly less than that price. He realized that his clients didn't actually care about the technology used to pump; they just cared that their fields got pumped. Given that he wanted to capture as many farmers as he could to recoup the costs of his equipment, Ibrahaim decided to price his service just beneath the competitive price — but way above his break-even.

Value Prop: For Nigerian healthcare providers, Chart Synergy makes electronic healthcare record-keeping better and cheaper than competing platforms by providing a high-quality system for patient data collection, storage, analysis and transmission.

PRIMARY Unit of Sale?

Per "seat," (per person using the app)

Pricing Strategy:

Reinvent the Value Exchange.

Why? Chart Synergy recognized that there was no competition that was exactly analogous to the service they offered. The most frequent "alternative" to Chart Synergy was paper-based record-keeping.

Therefore, Chart Synergy decided to use "willingness to pay" as its method to calculate its price per seat. They calculated that, if a hospital used Chart Synergy software, they could save themselves significant costs:

Physical costs of paper records: The average hospital needed to store paper patient records. Hospitals would spend on paper supplies, pens, photocopier ink, and electricity for paper-based record-keeping.

Personnel costs of paper records: Each hospital needed to employ one or two people just to create, maintain, and find all those pieces of paper — over and beyond the resources needed to update them with new patient information.

"Opportunity costs" of additional patient revenue lost to space for paper storage: Each hospital needed to set aside space in its building, typically allocating a separate room for that purpose. By freeing up that space by replacing paper records with digital records, hospitals could accommodate 4 new beds for patients, and bring in additional revenue per year by filling these beds.

Value Prop: For pregnant women, SonoCare offers more convenient, affordable, and accurate testing than expensive, remote, understaffed, under-equipped clinics with mobile diagnostic medical imaging services. **PRIMARY Unit of Sale?** Per test	**Pricing Strategy:** Price As Low As You Can (Profitably) Go **Why?** Dr. Moses of SonoCare realized that the main alternative to his services was usually no service at all. Since his true goal with his business was to help as many pregnant women as he could, Dr. Moses chose to keep prices as low as he could.
Your value prop: **What is *your* PRIMARY unit of sale?**	**Pricing Strategy?** **Why?**

Estimate the Average Revenue Per Unit

Revenue per unit is the amount of money your business brings in every time you sell one unit, whether this units is a single product or service.

Estimating Average Revenue Per Unit Using Price

If your unit of sale is something that shows up on a customer receipt — and doesn't vary between customers — in most cases the *price* of that unit will be your average revenue per unit. A good example of this is Basmalah Enterprises charging a flat fee of 22,000 Naira (about $60 USD) for every field that they irrigate. Since they don't discount, and don't charge more for larger fields or less for smaller fields, their average revenue per unit is 22,000 Naira.

Estimating Average Revenue Per Unit Using "Weighted Price"

For most businesses, though, calculating the average revenue per unit isn't as simple as just writing down the price. A slightly more complex example is Chart Synergy, the Electronic Patient Record company, which charges 4,000 Naira (about $11 USD) per seat. They also offer a "volume discount" of 10% for hospitals or clinics that purchase more than 20 seats at once. They've been in business for a while, so their data helps them estimate that about one in every four of their clients qualifies for a volume discount.

75% of clients pay a full 4,000 N, while 25% pay a discounted rate of 3,600 N.

The clients that pay full price, on average buy 5 units. Those that buy on discount, on average buy 20 units.

Avg Revenue per Unit = (full price) * (units at full price) * (% pay full price) + (discounted price) (# units at discounted price) * (% pay discounted price)

	% at price	avg units	weighted units
full	75%	5	3.75
discounted	25%	20	5

	price	weighted units	subtotal
full	4,000 N	3.75	15,000 N
discounted	3,600 N	5	18,000 N
		8.75	33,000 N

Chart Synergy thus calculated that its average revenue per unit is 33,000N / 8.75 units, or 3,771 N.

Estimating Average Revenue Per Unit Using a "Customer Basket"

Many, if not most, businesses have multiple products. For example, Chart Synergy (electronic healthcare record-keeping) could charge a fee to install their service, fees for monthly access, and incremental fees for any software changes they request. Grocery stores have many products on their shelves. Hair stylists charge different prices for women and men, for different hair lengths, and for different services. GreenPad Concepts (sanitary products) sometimes sells individual pads and other times sells packages of five or 10.

Each of these businesses has multiple items for sale, each with a different price. For these businesses, trying to model expenses by looking at each and every item, and each and every price, would get far too complicated to be an effective managerial tool for most entrepreneurs. (Or course, you'll eventually need to have an item-by-item understanding of what you're selling, at what price, and what your customers are buying, keeping, and using. However, right now, we're just trying to help you understand your business. It can help you to use a "customer basket" as your unit of sale and estimate the average revenue for that basket.

You want to pick a unit of sale that helps you forecast your future revenues — as well as your future costs. Entrepreneurs have told us it's far easier to see how they're doing if they pick a single unit of sale to model their business. They either pick one unit of sale (like "charge per field irrigated" or "charge per patient visit"), or else assess the unit of sale on an "average sale per customer" (sometimes referred to as a "shopping cart" or "basket") basis. For instance, a grocery store would average the receipts for each customer; its unit of sale would be the customer.

As an example of how a business can estimate the average revenue from a "customer basket," let's look at our favorite restaurant. It's open all day. It makes most of its money in the morning (from us, anyway) by selling coffee or tea and sometimes eggs and toast. If we go in the afternoon, we'll go buy a BLT sandwich and maybe a nice, cold, frothy Kolsch-style beer. In the early evening, customers like us would order snacks and a cocktail or two. At night, dinner and probably some wine. More cocktails. So, how would we estimate the average revenue from a customer visit?

We don't have their exact numbers, but we'll estimate. Let's say that, in the morning, most people spend about $5 on a coffee or a tea. Maybe 25% of the sales comes from these "coffee customers." Another 10% of the restaurant's daily customers will order a full breakfast. They'll pay another $12 for eggs, toast, and a side salad (in addition to $5 for their tea or coffee) – so about $17 in total. Then there's the lunch crowd, who probably account for another 25% of the restaurant's daily customers. They'll probably pay about $20 for lunch and a drink (say, juice or a milkshake). After lunch, until say 6pm, about 10% of the restaurant's daily customers come in for a beer and a snack, spending about $15. For the rest of the restaurant's day, most of its clients will come in and order dinner and a few drinks, for a total bill of about $25.

So: of the restaurant's daily customers, we have the following spend breakdown:

- ↔ 25% spend $5 ("coffee customers")
- ↔ 10% spend $17 ("full breakfast")
- ↔ 25% spend $20 ("lunch")
- ↔ 10% spend $15 ("beer and a snack")
- ↔ 30% spend $25 ("dinner and a few drinks")

This can help us get a spend breakdown of the entire day's basket:

Avg. revenue per customer = (.25x$5) + (.10x$17) + (.25x$20) + (.10x$15) + (.30x$25)

Average revenue per customer = $16.95

Using that calculation, we can estimate that the "average" customer spends about $17.

Some other examples of estimating the average revenue of other business are:

Value Prop:	Average Revenue per Unit:
For Nigerian farmers, Basmalah Enterprises pumps water less expensively than petrol-consuming generators, by using mobile solar power.	Basmalah Enterprises charges 22,000 Naira (about $60 USD) per field. Their CEO Ibrahim did the math and realized, at that price, he would be $10 less than most of his competition. This cheaper price would be hard for competition to match (given their cost structures) and would help him win business. He calculated that he could break even relatively easily at that price. He also decided not to discount – so his average revenue per unit is his price.
PRIMARY unit of sale?	
Per field pumped	
Pricing Strategy:	
Price slightly below competition, but at a break-even that makes sense	

Value Prop: For Nigerian healthcare providers, Chart Synergy makes electronic healthcare record-keeping better and cheaper than competing platforms by providing a high-quality system for patient data collection, storage, analysis and transmission.

PRIMARY unit of sale?

Per "seat," (per person using the app)

Pricing Strategy:

Reinvent the Value Exchange

Average Revenue per Unit:

Chart Synergy charges 4,000 Naira (about $11 USD) per seat. However, they also offer a "volume discount" of 10% for hospitals or clinics that purchase more than 20 seats at once — so Chart Synergy will need to "weight" their price to calculate average revenue per unit. They've been in business for a while so their data helps them estimate that about one out of every four clients qualifies for a volume discount. So, 75% of their clients pay the full 4,000 N, while 25% pay a discounted rate of 3,600 N.

As seen on page 163, the Average Revenue per Unit is 3,771N.

Value Prop:

For Seattle-based entrepreneurs, Origin Stories Coffee offers a meeting, work and event space specifically for people who are starting and running businesses and who want to interact with similar people.

PRIMARY unit of sale?

Per cup of coffee

Pricing Strategy:

Premium Pricing

Average Revenue per Unit:

The average cup of coffee at Origin Stories Coffee is $5 USD

What is your value prop?

What is your PRIMARY unit of sale?

What is your pricing strategy:

What is your Average Revenue per Unit?

Also write down your Average Revenue Per Unit in the #DoTheMath one-pager at the beginning of this section.

For Origin Stories Coffee
[E] Your Average Revenue per Unit of Sale = $5.00

For Basmalah
[E] Your Average Revenue per Unit of Sale = 22,000 N per field

For your business
[E] Your Average Revenue per Unit of Sale = _____

Make Money On Every Single Unit You Sell

For each product you sell, the "profit per unit" is the difference between the cost to produce that unit and the average revenue from that unit. (In fancy business schools, they call this term "Contribution Margin" instead of profit per unit.)

Profit per Unit = (Average Revenue Per Unit) − (Costs Per Unit)

The Profit per Unit is kind of a big deal. IT MUST ALWAYS BE POSITIVE. In the long term, you will NEVER be profitable if the amount you make per unit of sale is less than the amount it costs you to make it.

There are a handful of super-complicated businesses that can have a Profit per Unit on some products/services be slightly negative (for example a loss-leader like milk at the supermarket, or a piece of hardware like the Amazon Kindle), but those costs must ALWAYS be recovered elsewhere in the business. To try to keep this book as relevant as possible to you, we'll exclude these types of businesses for now.)

Luckily, the calculation is the simple subtraction of two terms you've already calculated.

For Origin Stories Coffee:

Profit per Unit = Average revenue − Cost per Unit

= [value of E] $5.00 - [value of D] $1.50

= $3.50

For Basmalah:

[F] Profit per Unit = Average revenue – Cost per Unit

11,500 N = [value of E] 22,000 N - [value of D] 10,500 N

Your turn:

What is your *cost per unit* (from the Figure Out Your Costs chapter)?

D: _____

What is your *average revenue per unit* (from the Average Revenue Per Unit chapter)?

E: _____

To determine your profit per unit, simply subtract [B] from [A]:

F: _____

Now you have the profit per unit. Write this down in the #DoTheMath one pager as below

[F] Profit per Unit = Average revenue – Cost per Unit

_____ = [value of E] _____ - [value of D] _____

Calculate Your Break-Even

In this chapter, we don't teach you accounting. We won't go into how to build a P&L, talk about your tax strategy, forecast your burn rate, or even help you understand your cash flow. Down the road, you'll need to think about all these things. In this chapter, however, we *DO* help you answer a simple, but VERY important question.

The question isn't "Can you build your solution?" We're sure you can. The question you need to ask, rather, is: "If you actually DO build your solution, will you be able to build a *profitable business*?" In other words, can you make enough money selling your solution to customers, in order to pay the costs you incurred making it (hopefully with something left over)?

To make your company profitable, you only have four variables to adjust: You can *sell more units*, e.g. by building a better product, or investing more money into advertising. You can *lower your variable costs*, e.g. by switching to lower-cost materials. You can *decrease your fixed costs*, e.g. by spending less on rent or on electricity. And you can also *adjust your price* (up — to capture more revenue per unit sold; or down, — to try to sell more units).

Notice how these four variables are related. If you invest to build a better product (to increase sales), your variable or fixed costs (or both) will go up. If you increase your price (to capture more revenue from each sale), your sales will likely decrease.

These variables all fit together into something called your "break even." To answer the question of "can I build a profitable business," you'll need to calculate your break even, and figure out if that number is realistic. Your business is "profitable" if the amount of money it brings in (within a time period, say a month), exceeds the

148

amount of money you've spent (in that same time period). If your costs are HIGHER than your revenue, you're losing money during that period. To understand what this actually means, LET'S DO SOME MATH. (Or not — if math makes you cringe, just skip this and the next page.)

We can write that exact same thing in the below equation.
Profit = (Total Revenue) − (Total Costs)

We can break down this equation even further, into its component parts.
Total Revenue = (Units Sold) x (Average Revenue Per Unit)
Total Cost = (Variable Costs) + (Monthly Fixed Costs)
Variable Costs = (Units Sold) x (Costs Per Unit)

We can rewrite THAT equation too:
Profit = ((Units Sold) x (Average Revenue Per Unit)) − (Variable Costs) − (Monthly Fixed Costs)

and that becomes
Profit = ((Units Sold) x (Average Revenue Per Unit)) − ((Units Sold) x (Costs Per Unit)) − (Monthly Fixed Costs)

We can rewrite THAT big mess as this...
Profit = (Units Sold) x ((Average Revenue Per Unit) − (Costs Per Unit)) − (Monthly Fixed Costs)

We can make the whole equation simpler:
Profit per Unit = (Average Revenue Per Unit) − (Costs Per Unit)

So this...
Profit = (Units Sold) x ((Average Revenue Per Unit) − (Costs Per Unit)) − (Monthly Fixed Costs)

...becomes this:

Profit = (Units Sold) x (Profit per Unit) – (Monthly Fixed Costs)

Using this equation, we can figure out your break-even. To do that, we want to figure out the answer to this question: "During this month, how many units do I have to sell, in order NOT TO LOSE MONEY?"

We do that by setting "business profit" to 0 in our equation:

0 = (Units Sold) x (Profit per Unit) – (Monthly Fixed Costs)

To answer our question, then, we just rearrange the terms of our equation:

0 = (Units Sold) x (Profit per Unit) – (Monthly Fixed Costs)

(Monthly Fixed Costs) = (Units Sold) x (Profit per Unit)

(Monthly Fixed Costs) / (Profit per Unit) = (Units Sold)

So — to answer the question: "During this month, how many units do I have to sell, in order NOT TO LOSE MONEY?"— we only need to solve this equation:

(Units Sold) = (Monthly Fixed Costs) / (Profit per Unit)

And (very luckily, ALMOST AS IF WE'VE PLANNED THIS), in the previous chapters, you've already compiled all the information you'll need to do just that. We can just plug in the information we need into the right spots in the equation.

For Origin Stories Coffee, it's this:

(Units Sold) = (Monthly Fixed Costs) / (Profit per Unit)

Cups of Coffee Sold = $20,300 / $3.50

Cups of Coffee Sold = 5,800

So we need to sell 5,800 cups of coffee a month just to break even. That's 5800/30 = 193 cups of coffee a day!

For Basmalah, it's this:

(Units Serviced) = (Monthly Fixed Costs) / (Profit per Unit)

58.43 = 672,000 N / 11,500 N

Each month, Ibrahim will need to service 59 number of fields to have a business rather than a hobby.

What about you? What does your break even look like?

[G] Monthly Break Even = Monthly fixed costs / Profit per Unit

_____ = [value of B] _____ / [value of F] _____

Each month (on average), you'll need to sell <Monthly Break Even> number of <Units of Sale> to have a business rather than a hobby.

Break-Even Example: Basmalah Enterprises

(Units Sold) = (Monthly Fixed Costs) / (Profit per Unit)

[A] **Unit of Sale** = Per Field

[B] **Monthly Fixed Costs** = 672,000 N

[C] **Investment Fixed Costs** = 4,781,000 N

[D] **Costs per Unit of Sale** = 10,500 N

[E] **Average Revenue per Unit of Sale** = 22,000 N (per field)

[F] **Profit per Unit** = Average revenue − Cost per Unit
11,500 N = [*value of E*] 22,000 N - [*value of D*] 10,500 N

[G] **Monthly Break Even** = Monthly fixed costs / Profit per Unit
58.43 fields = [*value of B*] 672,000 N / [*value of F*] 11,500 N

Each month (on average), Basmalah needs to **irrigate 59 fields** to break even.

Break-Even Example: Origin Stories Coffee

(Units Sold) = (Monthly Fixed Costs) / (Profit per Unit)

[A] **Unit of Sale** = Per Cup of Coffee

[B] **Monthly Fixed Costs** = $20,300

[C] **Investment Fixed Costs** = $20,725

[D] **Costs per Unit of Sale** = $1.50

[E] **Average Revenue per Unit of Sale** = $5.00 (per cup of coffee)

[F] **Profit per Unit** = Average revenue − Cost per Unit

$3.50 = [*value of E*] $5.00 - [*value of D*] $1.50

[G] **Monthly Break Even** = Monthly fixed costs / Profit per Unit

5,800 cups of coffee = [*value of B*] $20,300 / [*value of F*] $3.50

Each month (on average), Origin Stories needs to $5,800 sell cups of coffee to break even.

Break-Even: Your Turn!

This is the super-secret one-pager to figure out **IF YOU CAN BUILD A PROFITABLE BUSINESS from your idea!**

Here's the equation we'll use; you just need to fill in the blanks and do ONE calculation:

(Units Sold) = (Monthly Fixed Costs) / (Profit per Unit)

[A] **Your Unit of Sale** = _____

[B] **Your Monthly Fixed Costs** = _____

[C] **Your Investment Fixed Costs** = _____

[D] **Your Costs per Unit of Sale** = _____

[E] **Your Average Revenue per Unit of Sale** = _____

[F] **Profit per Unit** = Average revenue − Cost per Unit

_____ = [*value of E*] _____ - [*value of D*] _____

[G] **Monthly Break Even** = Monthly fixed costs / Profit per Unit

_____ = [*value of B*] _____ / [*value of F*] _____

Each month (on average), you'll need to sell **<Monthly Break Even>** number of **<Units of Sale>** to have a business rather than a hobby.

ACT III

How Will You Sell It?

YOU SURVIVED THE MATH SECTION! Hopefully, now you know if you have a hobby, a business or a non-profit. It's time for the most interesting part (one of us thinks, anyway) — *actually selling* your product or service. It might sound scary to start — will anyone actually pay for this thing? Never fear, though; we've got a 10-step formula to make this as simple as possible.

You're going to:

1. Take a deep breath
2. Reduce Variables
3. Tell your hero's story
4. Hustle for the help you need
5. Build a crew to help you
6. Brand your business
7. Manage your customers
8. Spread the word
9. Help your customers be your influencers
10. Launch the product

Ready? Let's go!

Take a Deep Breath

How are you feeling?
No really. What are your stress levels like?

> After the initial excitement of starting a business wears off, you're
> stuck with a lot of major realities of business plans and finances
> and customers and finding people to help you actually do this.

Do you feel overwhelmed? Afraid? Feeling like giving up? That's okay. IT'S TOTALLY NORMAL. We feel this way a lot and so do our 46 entrepreneurs.

Here is the solution. Take a deep breath. Do the self-care you need to do.

Some of our founders play video games and have been known to "clear an entire call of duty campaign in a night". Rosine Mwiseneza, from Rwanda takes long walks in the forest and breathes deeply. Dona takes a journal to a coffee shop and write out her troubles over way too many lattes. Then she texts her #TextableTribe (more on this later) with the key issues she's facing. They generally have great advice.

Jeremiah likes to go for a run, or head to the gym and lift heavy weights.

Many of our entrepreneurs take walks and call friends. What's your self-care ritual for the hard days?

Call a friend. Do some pushups. Drink some tea. Whatever that is. Take care of your body and mind...only then can you grow a Business.

Good? All right, let's do this!

Reduce Variables

It all started with incorrect information about effective birth control. This led to an unexpected teenage pregnancy, which in turn led to an illegal abortion and a young Kenyan woman named Sophie nearly losing her life.

Our team first met Irving Amukasa at the NexTech Africa conference in Nairobi, Kenya. Irving captivated us with his constant smile and his animated mannerisms. The man is in near-constant motion. Technology was Irving's first love. He'd started building bots before bots became a household word.

Irving was in college when he heard Sophie's story, which impacted him deeply. A close friend of his, Beverly confirmed that this was indeed the case for many people she knew.

A lack of sexual health education or reliable information leads to 7.3 million unplanned births every year, and young women are especially impacted. Many abandon their dreams to care for their unplanned children. Because of societal shame, they're often shunned by their families. Most of these pregnancies could have been prevented with accurate information rather than myths and folklore related to pregnancy.

Irving devised an ingenious solution for this global challenge — he threw tech at the problem. He realized that talking about sex with other people was taboo in his country. But there were few social norms around talking about sex with a bot! A bot could give accurate and useful advice, safely and discreetly.

And so, came the birth of SophieBot — a friendly, geeky automated online bot that answers questions about sexual health. As people ask questions, Irving finds the answers and adds both the questions and answers to the existing SophieBot dataset.

Irving had a vision that SophieBot would handle objective questions, but he also wanted there to be a forum on their website and app where people could anonymously discuss subjective topics.

The SophieBot part worked great and within a few weeks they had hundreds of users asking useful questions. The forums… not as much. They quickly deteriorated into inappropriate discussions, driving away all productive conversation.

Irving realized the MOST important part of his business was the bot, not the forums. He decided to do an ancient software engineer trick: reduce variables. Instead of trying to solve all of the problems at once, for his version one, he would really solve SophieBot and then solve the forum problem in version two. You can find SophieBot at http://sophiebot.ml/

To make SophieBot successful, Irving had to Reduce Variables…as in reduce the number of things that he was trying to do at the same time.

Reducing variables can be an incredibly heart-breaking moment for an entrepreneur. This is when the reality of the business doesn't match the vision — YET. This can happen for a variety of reasons: the technology isn't ready; the finances don't support it; or you don't have the right member of your team to implement it.

For the first version, we highly recommend you think about the core dimensions of your business (the ones you defined all the way back in the Fit Your Solution into Gowan's World chapter). By now, you should have enough customers that you know what aspects of your solution are most relevant to them.

If the variable you need to reduce is not a core dimension,
remove it! You can always add it back in later once
you're really delivering on your core dimensions.

Prima Dona Example

Dona had a particular heartbreak around this section. Her original vision for Prima Dona was that everything would be reversible. This would help people get more out of the single garment AND reduce waste and space in someone's closet. Unfortunately, creating reversible garments in quite difficult. There are two kinds of fabric to think about and two zippers on each item. The set of samples that were reversible were not easy to wear.

What did she do? Reduced variables. She kept in mind that "reversible" was NOT one of the key reasons people were buying Prima Dona. Instead they were buying garments because they were "high impact" and "helped them stand out". This could be done with non-reversible clothing.

Reluctantly, Dona let go of this idea for version one. It was hard and she had to take the time to mourn the loss. Reversibles will come back to Prima Dona someday---just not for version one.

Boxes and Foxes Example

Jeremiah also had to re-think his business, when confronted with the realities of actually TRYING to start it.

His original vision for Boxes and Foxes was that he would be able to visit each of his founders, shadow them around so he could actually see the inner workings of their business, and then be able to offer immediately-useful, targeted insights that might not even be exactly the initial question that the founder had come in with.

However, after testing out this idea with a few entrepreneurs, he realized that he'd never be able to make this work at scale. In the first place, Boxes and Foxes is his side hustle. His day job isn't exactly the sort of job he can just drop at a moment's notice, to be able to take off to visit a new founder. For example, his Hero, Rachel, lives in Amsterdam. Her co-founder, Jessica, lives in Zambia. EVEN FOR HIS HERO, Jeremiah couldn't execute on this idea.

What did he do? Reduced variables. He remembered that "visit me in person and giving me insights into my business even I might not have thought of" was NOT one of the main reasons startup founders might want to work with him. Instead, most startup founders knew EXACTLY what the highest-value problem they faced, and could just TELL Jeremiah that, over Skype, or WhatsApp, or a phone call.

Sadly, Jeremiah let go of this idea for version one. (Maybe sometime he'll get to visit Jessica in Zambia.) Not this time, though.

Now it's your turn

After doing your finances and building your team, are there any parts of your business you need to let go of — for now? Write them down. Mourn them. Bring them back another day.

Tell Your Hero's Story

Caleb Ndaka is trying to buy a van and a few more laptops.

Years ago, when he was in college at JKUAT (Jomo Kenyatta University of Agriculture and Technology) in Nairobi, Kenya, Caleb and his friends had a conversation. They decided they wanted to be more impactful on society to help those who were less fortunate. They realized they all had laptops and a bit of pocket money, something the average person in Kenya did not have. On a whim, they took a road trip to a school in a village with no access to computers. Once there, they spent a few days training the students on computer basics. Their students were awestruck at these lessons and were quickly able to pick up the skills. Caleb was surprised to see such quick progress, realizing he could have a real impact on his country with this work. That was the day Caleb's business Comp Camp was born.

Caleb and his team of four made a quick promo video for Comp Camp which they shared across their network. Suddenly, they received over 50 requests to do similar camps all over East Africa. Caleb hesitated — he was a student and was no expert in training others. While he and his friends had managed to find twenty laptops, they didn't have proper transportation. They'd need to move from one village to the next —be it hitchhike, use public transportation, or even walk — carrying the machines in battered, overloaded backpacks. This was a hard life.

However, requests for these camps kept coming in from all over Kenya. The demand made it clear to Caleb that he'd found the work he needed to do. He set up an online form to capture the requests. Then he followed up with a survey to establish:

1. Need (they wanted to help first-time computer users)
2. Support from the local community (to build the relationships that would make the training successful)
3. Location (once they had identified which villages they wanted to go to, they could group them into trips to minimize the travel)

When we met Caleb during the fellowship program, we were blown away by his charisma and conviction. Here was a young man who could use his tech skills to get a traditional software engineering job or use his amazing stage presence to be a theater actor. He could have left the problem of tech illiteracy in his country to someone else. But, Caleb was not having any of that. He's genuinely excited about the future of the communities they served and loves what the kids create, even after just a day of computer training.

Caleb's biggest challenge was figuring out how to make an income from this work. He also wanted to scale, to grow his business so they could reach more people.

While doing the fellowship program. Caleb and team realized that instead of simply training kids in schools (which would take a very long time and result in no income), they needed to train adults to support the kids. This is an approach that's also known as "train the trainer."

That day, Comp Camp became for kids... and the adults who love them. Since then, they have been working with two types of adult trainers: Campus trainers and Community trainers.

Campus trainers are drawn from universities from across East Africa. They're required to bring a laptop to participate and pay a fee. So far over 800 have signed up for this training because after learning these skills, they can go off an seek a career training others to use computers.

Community trainers are different — their goal is to support their local town or village in technology. They work with Caleb to identify where to do the training based on the availably of space with both furniture and electricity. This is harder than it seems! They pay a fee on behalf of the community in exchange for using Caleb's laptops to learn the lessons.

Caleb is already seeing the impact of this work. Last year during elections, one of the requirements was computer literacy since the elections were digitized. Twenty of Comp Camp students worked with the elections commission as clerks to help count the votes.

Caleb was looking to raise money for twenty more laptops and a van so that he could split his team in half and cover twice the ground. However, throwing out a lot of facts and figures looking for people willing to donate to the cause wasn't doing the trick. We helped him craft a story of who specifically he had built Comp Camp for.

Ten-year-old Bernice was the best coder in Kids Comp Camp in Nairobi, Kenya. Unfortunately, Eunice, Bernice's mother didn't understand the value of this "Komputya Mashini". She demanded that her daughter spend the time working in the fields instead. Caleb Ndaka, founder of Comp Camp, realized that Eunice didn't understand the value of technology because she hadn't been exposed to it in her own life. Caleb decided to teach Eunice how to use the internet, teaching her to file her taxes online, mandatory for her job. At that moment, Comp Camp became for kids... and the adults who love them. You can find us at http://kidscompcamp.com/

Caleb could have told his story this way, or he could have said, "Comp Camp offers coding classes to kids and adults. Both Bernice and her mother Eunice are taking the classes and are successful at them."

Which story is more compelling? Of course, the first one! We are human. We love stories. Stories are as old as the campfire and as new as the tweet. You need to tell your story in the most compelling way possible featuring your hero.

The Hero's Journey

Listing out all the options and features of your product is not going to move people to buy or use your product. Know what might? Hearing a story about someone who is now more successful or happier because they used your product.

Prima Dona Example

Ioana Tanase is going to be giving an important speech at a STEM (Science, Technology, Engineering, Math) conference in February in San Francisco—all about how students could network their way into their dream jobs. There would be hundreds of students there—many of whom Ioana wanted to hire. Ioana wanted to make sure she formed a very human connection with the attendees—to show them that she was a real person, not someone nameless and faceless at Microsoft.

How could she get across the point that all kinds of people worked at Microsoft: technical, artistic, and both. She wanted her image to be professional, but also unique. She also didn't want to spend a lot of money on an outfit—at least not on generic designer fashion that looked ordinary. She wanted something that would help her feel professional and confident at this industry event, but also feel creative and cool at the shoe-design course she was taking on weekends. What to do? Half the city wore the same clothes. She definitely didn't want to be one of the crowd.

Enter Prima Dona. The bright, stand-out print and professional shape helped Ioana stand out in the crowd, be seen as a leader AND gave her an excellent talking point for when someone complimented her. "Thank you! It was made by a tailor in Kenya."

The feedback from Ioana? "On days I need to put on my armor and go and conquer whatever lies ahead? Those are the days I need Prima Dona."

Boxes and Foxes Example

Rachel Elsinga has finally done it. She quit her job at the Big Investment Bank she's worked at for nearly a decade. She's working to create a business with one of her closest friends, Jessica. Their mission is to answer a question they've seen over and over again — and one that no one else is willing or able to tackle: How can organizations build products and services that are truly inclusive, specifically for women? These are decades-old problems like the fact that seatbelts and airbags are designed to protect men in case of car accidents. Together, the two women started Equilo.org, an organization to hack gender equality and SOLVE THIS PROBLEM FOR GOOD.

The main issue that Rachel has run into is a common one for startup founders: how to raise funds to pay for the infrastructure they need to build? There are a lot of potential options to consider. They could apply for grants, from big NGOs, foundations, and the UN. They could crowdfund, and hope that their friends and network could help them raise money. They could "side-hustle," and work second and third jobs to fund Equilo. There are a bunch of other options, too. Which to choose?

One of Jeremiah's superpowers is his broad and diverse network, from his decades of unique work experiences. He can call on his network to help talk through problems related to technology, marketing, PR, operations and such.

He worked closely with Rachel, and was able to talk through with her the several options. He provided her with a framework to think about the challenge. Based on their work together, she feels like she knows exactly which course to pursue: she's going for funding through grants from foundations. This option TOTALLY might not work. They might not receive any grant funding. But, even if that first attempt doesn't work, she knows which options she's going to try next. Thanks, Boxes and Foxes! ☺

You will need to tell your story to attract potential customers, partners, funding, anything. You'll notice we've started every chapter in this book with a real story featuring a real hero. This was not by accident.

It's time for you to do the same thing. Remember, when we politely asked you to choose a real-life hero? It's time to write down their story (or some other customer who you have impacted with your product) in a way that makes them compelling. How do you do that? One simple way is telling your story in the form of The Hero's Journey — the way authors and screenwriters write most of the classic western world books and movies you know. For each of our entrepreneur stories, we've used the format below.

Think about the problem they're facing and how your product is the solution to it.

The Hero's Journey

- ∞ Who's the hero of the story and what's their ordinary world like?
- ∞ What's the problem they've encountered?
- ∞ What's holding them back from solving the problem?
- ∞ How did they find you?
- ∞ How did your business help them?
- ∞ How's their life better?

Hustle All Day

We always tell people that our technology is not saving lives... but our customers sure as heck are.

Throughout her life, 18-year-old Ange Uwambajimana of Kigali, Rwanda had always cared for her younger brother Saga who suffered from epilepsy. Saga spent most of his young life in hospitals, attached to an IV drip. One day, Ange left his hospital room and walked down the hall to buy him some juice. Suddenly, she heard him screaming. She rushed back to his room and found an awful sight — Saga's IV drip was empty and there was blood back-flow in the tube! Ange screamed for the nurse, who came running to refill the IV drip. The nurse told Ange that she'd quite possibly saved her brother's life.

Once past the emergency, Ange learned this was a structural problem. In many hospitals, there was no formal process to monitor IV drips other than a nurse occasionally passing by the room. There were simply not enough nurses in Rwanda to keep an eye on every IV. The risks were high — infections and possible death. Saga's life would perpetually be in danger.

Many patients in these situations are dependent on their family members. But managing patients' fluid and electrolyte levels is a critical, challenging, and stressful task for anyone — especially a non-medical professional. Serious problems such air embolisms can occur if the observer forgets to change the IV at the correct time, or over-infuses the patient. This can have fatal consequences.

Ange realized that her brother's case was incredibly common. She saw there was a far bigger problem in her home country of Rwanda — so she decided to tackle it.

She enrolled in a computer science program at a university in her city to learn the skills she needed.

During our fellowship, she started working on a prototype for an IoT (Internet of Things) project. She wanted to build an automated IV drip solution which would monitor IV drips and alert nurses when they were running low. Her teacher's assistant was so moved by her story that he joined her team along with two of her other classmates. By using an automatic monitoring valve, they've built an accurate and efficient solution. Their device monitors fluid administration and delivers the fluid in controlled amounts. When the fluid runs out, IV Drip Alert pings the nurses' room.

Ange knew she was building for one — her brother. To scale, though, she needed the hospital to test it on other people like him. How could she convince the hospital to give her a chance?

Ange used an ancient entrepreneurship skill: hustle — the art of getting what you need without the other person feeling taken advantage of.

Her first step was to get super-clear on what she wanted.

IV Drip Alert Example

ଓ What do you want, and why?

"I've created an automated IV drip solution and want to test it in a Rwandan hospital so a situation like my brother's never happens again."

Her next step was to figure out who could help her and what their currency — the thing that they care about; the thing that makes them "tick" — is.

170

ભ Who's the person you need to influence? (Remember, you're building for ONE human being)

The human is Tana, the hospital administrator where Saga is hospitalized.

ભ What do THEY want? (If you don't know this, you CANNOT influence them)

Ange befriended some of the nursing staff and found out that Tana has two goals: reduce costs in the next year (from both lawsuits and other maintenance costs) and to prevent death from medical negligence.

ભ What words do they use to talk about their goals?

The best way for Ange to find out all of this information was to observe Tana working with the hospital staff as she gave instructions and made schedules.

She mentioned over the over the term "prevent negligent death" as a main goal for the whole staff.

Other ways for you to do this research is through online research such as LinkedIn profiles, any articles or interviews they have done. Otherwise, you should talk to people who know them personally and professionally. A third option is to talk to others in similar roles to really perfect the pitch to influence them before you approach your target.

ભ What is the overlap of your goals and their goals (if any)

Prevent negligent death.

ભ If no overlap, how can you help them? (focus on helping THEM first, rather than getting your ask in — once they like you and respect you, they will want to help you)

There is overlap.

Once Ange had the information and found out a nurse's pay per hour as they monitored IV drips, she realized she could save them 10% of cost every week since the nurse would not need to check on the IV. The alerting system would proactively notify nurses.

Here's the proposal she made to them:

ଓ The Intro (showing them you get where they are coming from)

I know you have a goal of reducing costs in this hospital this year — while also preventing negligent death.

ଓ The Play (showing them you have something to offer that helps meet THEIR goal)

I've created a prototype that automatically alerts nurses when an IV needs attention. This reduces their time and your overall cost of staff time by 10% in one week.

ଓ The Pitch (your ask--said in their own words)

I'd love to know if you're interested in testing this in your hospital so you can reduce your costs while preventing negligent death.

And guess what? THIS WORKED! Ange was able to convince six Rwandan hospitals to test her device.

Prima Dona Example

ଓ What do you want or need?

Dona wants her Prima Dona garments to be showcased somewhere physically so she could gauge interest, get feedback and spread the word about her new collection. Plus, many people need to see and try on a garment in person before deciding to buy.

ଓ Who's the person you need to influence?

She needs to influence Ambika Singh, the CEO of Armoire.Style, a Seattle-based clothing rental service. She needs Armoire to both carry her designs as well as host a pop-up so people can see the styles in real life. Armoire often hosts events where they bring a sample set of their clothing to people's homes or offices.

ଓ What do THEY want?

Ambika wants people to rent clothing instead of buying or contributing to the fast fashion industry. She wants more customers using Armoire.

ଔ What words do they use? (You need to really research to make sure you understand their currency)

> *Women don't really need to buy clothes every time the season changes, or they go on vacation, or start a new job.*

ଔ What is the overlap of your goals and their goals (if any)?

> *Both Dona and Ambika want to reduce people buying clothes every time the season changes, they go on vacation or start a new job.*

ଔ Even if no overlap, how can you help them anyway? (Focus on helping THEM first, rather than getting your ask in. They're more likely to offer help.)

> *There is an overlap and Dona can help Ambika by creating unique styles that are only available via Armoire.*

Once you have this info, here is the pitch you can use:

ଔ The Intro (showing them you get where they are coming from). Use THEIR words exactly.

> *I know you have a goal of reducing people's dependency on buying new clothes for every occasion*

ଔ The Play (showing them you have something to offer that helps meet THEIR goal)

> *I've created a line of clothing that's hand-crafted by tailors in Kenya and Nigeria one at a time. These are clothes that are for ALL aspects of their life. Professional shapes for a business environment, but prints that are too fun to just keep at work.*

ଔ The Pitch (your ask — said in their own words)

> *Would you be interested in me adding this to Armoire as an exclusive, not available anywhere else option? Maybe we can have these Prima Dona styles showcased at your next Armoire party?*

Boxes and Foxes Example

ଓ What do you want or need?

Jeremiah needs help spreading the word about his service to startup founders who can use his help.

ଓ Who's the person you need to influence?

He needs to influence Amy Nelson, who is the founder of the female forward co-working startup The Riveter. She has an incredibly broad network of entrepreneur friends all over the world — many of them customers of The Riveter. They would be GREAT customers for Jeremiah.

ଓ What do THEY want?

Amy wants to build a global movement to redefine the future of work so that ambitious, independent folks gain a seat at the table.

ଓ What words do they use? (You need to really research to make sure you understand their currency)

There's a lot of money to be made by taking women seriously.

Has a love of tackling big issues

Being an entrepreneur doesn't require a special degree. Being an entrepreneur is taking out all the tools you have in your toolkit and figuring out how to use them.

It's really hard to make the pivot into entrepreneurship, but the hard part is that we convince ourselves that we can't do it.

As long as you have enough hustle, you can do it.

She wants to help ambitious, independent folks.

Wants to make sure everyone has a seat at the table.

Women get only 2% of VC dollars despite starting businesses at a rate of five times more than men.

The maternal wall — take it down brick by brick

Companies with strong female leadership generate higher returns.

Startups with at least 1 female founder perform 63% than ones with all male.

Grow from an idea to a trusted community.

Give up on perfectionism every day

Who you know is everything.

Words they DON'T use:

Balance or boundaries when talking about juggling entrepreneurship and parenting

ᦉ What is the overlap of your goals and their goals (if any)?

Both Jeremiah and Amy want to help founders, especially people who come from a non-traditional background such as women and minorities.

ᦉ Even if no overlap, how can you help them anyway?

There is an overlap, but Jeremiah can help Amy by offering Boxes and Foxes consulting to members of The Riveter at a discount. He will also propose the idea of hosting office hours at one of the Seattle Riveter locations once a month and potentially once a quarter in LA.

Once you have this info, here is the pitch you can use:

ᦉ The Intro (showing them you get where they are coming from). Use THEIR words exactly.

I know you have a goal of helping ambitious entrepreneurs have a seat at the table.

ᦉ The Play (showing them you have something to offer that helps meet THEIR goal)

I've created a consulting service to help non-traditional startup founders achieve their business goals based on my decades of experience on Wall Street, the tech industry, and emerging markets.

ᦉ The Pitch (your ask — said in their own words)

Would you be interested in me offering members of the Riveter access to this service at a steep discount as well as me setting up office hours at the CapHill Riveter once a month, and potentially the LA location a few times a year?

You've likely reached the point in your entrepreneurial journey where you need to convince some other person to do something to benefit your business. Whether it's mentorship, funding, someone to be a co-founder or a journalist to create some media hype for you, you need to influence a person who previously saw no reason to care about your business.

My friend, it's time to hustle.

Let's look at an opposite example.

Have you ever gotten this kind of email or message?

Hi. I'm working on an emerging tech platform and wanted some time from you to discuss.

We've sure gotten this email. A lot.

99% of "cold connection" attempts — meaning from people you don't know or know well — are annoying. This was definitely in the 99% region.

Why would anyone respond to that? This person just searched LinkedIn, found someone with "emerging tech" in their history and cold contacted with no context of making the person they are reaching out to feel valued or appreciated.

There are two truths of hustle that will help you:

1. People will help people they like

2. People like people who make them feel understood and appreciated

---

To leverage these two truths, you need to be able to answer the following questions:

- What do you want or need? (You know this very clearly)
- Who's the person you need to influence? (Remember, you're building for ONE human being)
- What do THEY want? (If you don't know this, you CANNOT influence them)
- What words do they use? (You need to really research to make sure you understand their currency)
- What is the overlap of your goals and their goals (if any)?

ଔ If no overlap, how can you help them anyway? (Focus on helping THEM first, rather than getting your ask in. They're more likely to offer help.)

Once you have this info, here is the pitch you can use:

ଔ The Intro (showing them you get where they are coming from)
ଔ The Play (showing them you have something to offer that helps meet THEIR goal)
ଔ The Pitch (your ask — said in their own words)

What if the person says they are too busy or not interested? It happens. Don't get discouraged. We have another strategy for you. Who is someone they have mentored in the past? Who works on their team? Who is someone with similar values and skills?

We used to be obsessed with the idea of being mentored by superstar people whose videos, writings and speeches we hung on to like gold. But then, we realized we'd get similar benefit by meeting also with people who are their employees, mentees and practitioners. After all, these are people who have tried the superstars' techniques and now have their own advice to give on these matters.

Lesson learned: figure how to learn from the mentees/practitioners rather than the stars. Mentees are likely looking to build their own brands and will appreciate the support.

Who can you talk to with similar values and skills as the superstars, but is more accessible?

Build Your Team

A few months after his daughter was born, Andres Korin was up at 3am feeding her with a bottle when the "why him" moment hit. "I was sitting there holding her and sort of staring off into the corner. I started thinking about the financial impact a child has on their family," he told us. "Parents are doing the very thing that we as a species are designed to be doing – having kids. And yet, we're being penalized for it!"

Andres and his family live in London, which has excellent public policies to support parents. Even there, however, the financial challenges of parenthood can be daunting. According to Andres, most parents find the first two years of a baby's life to be the most expensive because of increased shopping costs, low parental pay and the high cost of childcare. Seeking to make ends meet, many people like Andres' wife, Astrid, head back to work earlier than they'd like. But even this might not solve the problem. In many cases, childcare is so expensive (particularly if you have more than one child) that it's not even financially worthwhile to go back to work.

Thinking about the challenges of parenthood, Andres came up with the idea of StorkCard, a "socially-responsible lending platform" that provides affordable and flexible financing to parents during this expensive period.

StorkCard helps them cover their costs during parental leave and pay for childcare after they return to work.

StorkCard became Andres' side hustle. He would work late on nights and weekends when the house was quiet. He bought a separate laptop and a copy of Office to avoid using any of his employer's resources. He toiled diligently to make his idea a reality — he created value props, elevator pitches, pro forma P&Ls. Developed plans for marketing, operations, and fundraising. Drew up a risk assessment framework.

In many ways, Andres had exactly the skills he'd need to build out this solution. His decade's experience in lending and financial structuring would be crucial to StorkCard. Responsibly lending money to people can be complicated. "In a way," Korin says, "debt can be either good or bad depending on the exact circumstances." Andres compares the financial structuring side to plumbing – you need to get it right the first time, but then you never have to think about it again. Both skills would be essential to StorkCard — and Korin had become proficient in both in his current job.

He realized, however, he wouldn't be able to pull off the entire project on his own. To StorkCard he could bring hard work, a solid background in the space, a deep understanding of the problem he was seeking to solve, and a vision for much of the solution. But he needed more; he'd need a technical partner.

For his project to succeed, Andres knew that he'd need a website or an app, in order to collect information from prospective parents, do some initial risk processing, hand off the request to back-end providers, and sustain a system that would bill and pay. Despite his proficiency in Excel, Andres didn't have the skills needed for this.

His solution sketch looked like this:

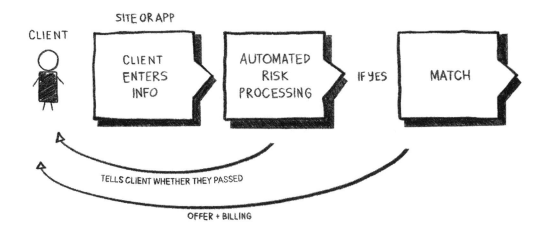

Andres spent a LOT of time trying to narrow his focus. He took half a programming class on Python, and paid for one in Java (which he still hasn't started but hopes to "soon"). He says now that he'd spent less time on programming classes and even more time researching things he didn't know, he could clearly visualize 80% of the business. He knew exactly how the end solution would look and feel to the user. He could envision what the back-end financial transactions would need to be. For him, the 20% unknown parts of the solution were the back-end tech to process risk, the search to find providers, making the offer and the billing process.

At this point, he'd been developing the concept for about 10 months, so had a good sense what the business was about. He was willing to commit a substantial part of his future to this endeavor. He asked himself if he wanted to go it alone and hire a vendor to do the tech work, or if he wanted a real partner. He realized he worked best in collaborative environments so he wanted to bring in a true co-founder. Even though it was something he'd spent a lot of time on, he decided that he wanted an equal partner to help bring it to life and to help him grow it alongside him. He needed to build his team.

We've spoken to hundreds of entrepreneurs all around the world, at hackathons and conferences, business schools and incubators. We've talked to enough founders to realize something surprising about Andres' question — his is not just a London or a Silicon Valley or a Seattle question.

It's a universal question: how do I build my team?

We think you've probably asked yourself this question as well, and it's the reason why you're reading this. Know this: YOU ARE NOT ALONE.

In this chapter, we will assume you need a technical co-founder, but it really applies to anyone: a financial co-founder, a marketing co-founder, a mentor, etc.

Founders worldwide need to find partners with skills to complement their own strengths. We've met people everywhere from Phnom Penh, Cambodia to San Jose, Costa Rica to Kathmandu, Nepal to Detroit, Michigan — and the most common thing they've told us is this: *I've got a great idea. I understand my potential clients and their needs pretty well. I can sketch out the process flow. I have some ideas for an MVP. I know how to make a P&L. I have a fair idea how to build out my marketing plans, and how operations might look. I just don't know technology. How can I find someone to help?*

Building your team is critical.

There are zero people in the world who can do all the parts of a business alone and do them WELL.

To build your team, you need to answer the following questions just as Andres had to.

ଓ *What do you need help on?*

Let's go back to your boxes-and-arrows of your Sketch the Solution chapter. For each of those boxes, what do you think the tech is? A database? A matching algorithm? Which other apps or services do something similar? Do these thought exercises — do as much work as possible to understand EXACTLY what you think you need. Search engines, Stack Overflow, and Wikipedia are your friends here. Take classes online or in person. Ask for advice from your network. You don't need a formal tech background for any of these.

Remember that "someone with tech skills" is a pretty broad category. That description can fit someone who deploys security updates to thousands of machines in an enterprise, someone who keeps a web service running 24/7, someone who writes Android apps, someone who designs simple websites, someone who's a back-end web developer (dev), someone who understands machine learning models and a thousand other variations.

Make a list of things that you think your tech co-founder should know how to do. NOW you're ready to go look for someone.

❧ *How can I add value?*

Remember the rule of hustle, you must first provide value. The first step is to understand the startup landscape in your city or town, understand what value you can add and then give, give, give. The technical people are not going to show up at your house asking to write code for you. You need to do this by going to where the technical people are and providing them some sort of value.

Most cities have some sort of startup scene, whether it's Startup Weekends, Startup Grind, classes at WeWork, hackathons or meet-up groups at local universities. If there really is nothing where you live, then start one. You are definitely not the only person who wants to start their own business. You need to start building your network face-to-face with these people who are also interested in starting their own businesses. Every single one of our East Africa entrepreneurs met their co-founders either at university or a local startup event. A good way to find local interested people is via the Lean Startup Circles.

Recently, we were reading the Slack channel of a local virtual reality hackathon. There was an entire thread with people looking for jobs or co-founders. You need to be aware of the conversations going on with people who want similar things as you. A very easy way to get involved is to join a team during a hackathon (you do NOT need to be technical to do this — often what's sorely lacking from these teams is a "storyteller" or a project manager). We know many people whose co-founders were originally members of their hackathon teams.

Do some research into what other entrepreneurs are looking for. A great way to do this is to join a Facebook group for entrepreneurs. One we have loved and referred many people to is Entrepreneur Hustle, which does an excellent job of sharing advice, resources and opportunities.

Once you know this, attend, volunteer or even organize an event with these topics as the talks. Influence companies and organizations to sponsor the space, the food, speakers and everything else you need. Invite the teachers of local coding bootcamps and local venture capital (VC) firms to your event. Invite founders of local startups to speak and share their stores. Invite a local startup's CTO to keynote your event. Ask all these people to spread the word to their networks. Remember, these people probably know more technical people than you do.

Spread the word among entrepreneur clubs at community colleges and universities. Remember, many young people want to be their own boss. Get the word out on every online startup channel in your area: Facebook, Twitter, Meetup, etc. Suddenly, you're not just a participant in the startup scene, you're a leader.

Andres got involved in the London startup scene and had a LOT of conversations. Every new conversation, even if the person didn't end up being a good fit, was helpful. It helped Andres broaden his network. The advice he found the most helpful was simple: fail small, fail quickly.

He went to a speed pitch session to observe and before he knew it, he was up there giving his pitch along with very specifically what he needed. He felt completely unprepared, but a guy named Bruce Pannaman came up to him to congratulate him on his pitch. Bruce seemed to "get" Andres' social mission and purpose. The two agreed to meet up for coffee a few days later.

○ৄ *What is the test?*

It should never be, "I just met you; now just sign this equity agreement." You want to work with someone you like and trust, hopefully shares the same vision: the deal has to work well for both people. You should become friends first. Offer your help. Ask for their advice. If you find them helpful, then approach the idea of co-founding something together.

Andres was clear from the get-go that this should be a learning experience for both Bruce and him. Andres wanted to spend a minimum amount of money getting the MVP up and running to learn. That way, even if they parted ways, both of them would benefit. Bruce, in turn, was very respectful of Andres' vision and wanted to make sure it was a partnership from the beginning.

The two spent three months setting up an initial website. Andres led the design, and Bruce led the back-end development. During this time, Andres asked Bruce for ideas on a marketing plan. (Since neither were marketing experts, it was a good, low-risk, way of seeing how the two worked together). Andres also taught Bruce a bit about finance, something Bruce had no experience with. They tried to teach each other their respective expertise as if they were explaining something to a three-year old. By doing so, they were able to ensure the other fully understood the approach they were taking.

The first big test of their partnership came when they surveyed 400 mothers in the UK, in order to support assumptions around their problem. Together, they went through the survey questions to make sure each one made sense. They also attended a small business networking event and organized a booth. Here, Andres got to see Bruce act as a real partner who was invested in the problem, rather than a "techie for hire." He got to see Bruce in sales mode, enthusiastically pitching their idea to strangers. Andres realized then that this guy had been the right choice far beyond just his technical acumen. In Bruce, he'd found someone who could deliver above and beyond his core competencies. Andres now had a true thought partner, someone to bounce ideas off of, someone who was able to turn on the sales mode. On top of code, Bruce would be crucial in manning the customer service calls. In short, Andres had found his partner.

℞ *What next?*

What does the partnership look like? Salary? Equity? After this, what other help do you need? Return to the first question. Now you have doubled your network!

For Andres and Bruce, they knew they needed help with branding and the user experience of their website. Bruce was a back-end developer and a data scientist, but he'd always made it clear he was not good at front-end user experience. Andres is color-blind, so both agreed they needed more help one some of the design elements.

Today, after participating in the Finance Innovation Lab's social enterprise incubator, Andres and Bruce are in talks with investors and the UK regulator ahead of the imminent launch of StorkCard. They also looking for potential employers who are interested in using StorkCard as a cost-effective way to enhance their existing benefits package. If you're in the UK and are starting a family, look for StorkCard (www.storkcard.com).

Boxes and Foxes Example

ℰ What do you NOT know about building your product?

Jeremiah would like to reach beyond his immediate network to find customers who are non-traditional outside of the US. To do this, he needs to use social media marketing strategies better. This is not something he's done in the past, so he'll need some help.

ℰ What do you need help on most urgently?

Social media marketing — especially in emerging markets or ones used by scrappy fledging companies.

ℰ How can you add value in your ecosystem?

He can help startups in some areas of their businesses, such as the marketing segmentation and economics.

ℰ What is the test you can do with your would-be co-founder/partner/ mentor?

Do an ad campaign to gain interest and drive attention to a landing page.

Now it's your turn

In your workbook, answer the following questions:

ଓ *What do you NOT know about building your product?*

ଓ *What do you need help on most urgently?*

ଓ *How can you add value in your ecosystem?*

ଓ *What is the test you can do with your co-founder?*

Brand Your Idea

Logos! Colors! Catchy slogans!

What do you think of when you hear these words? If you're like 99% of the world, you think "brand". And yes, you'd be right. Back in the day, a company's brand had to do with their logo, the colors of their website and their slogan. Think the Coca-Cola logo, the Nike "Just Do It" slogan.

However, in modern times, a company's brand is not only all of the above, but more importantly related to their purpose, reputation and the experience they provide. If a company's behavior does not match up to their brand, customers lose faith.

> Brand is the promise you make your customers. If you don't
> tell people what that promise is, they will make it up.

People are very creative animals.

Brand is the relationship between you & your customers. You must build up so much good credibility with them that if you mess up, you might get a second chance.

Your company's brand is people's impression about your business. It's what they think and feel about your business.

Their perception is what drives them to either buy from you or not buy. The good news is that you can help shape their perception by the story you tell about your business.

Irving Amukasa, the CEO of SophieBot, the sexual health bot is the master of brand. He has built a fantastic team and has marketed his business spectacularly. Marie Stopes International ("Africa's Planned Parenthood") and Liverpool MCT are interested in using SophieBot. He recently appeared on *Lion's Den* – "Kenya's *Shark Tank*" – where two investors were keen to help take his business further. SophieBot now has 150 active users and answers 300 new questions every month.

During our time working with our 46 entrepreneurs, we found Irving to have created the strongest brand across the board. We'll use SophieBot to illustrate some examples of brand questions you should answer for your own business. Irving's answers are below. What are yours?

Your vision: what is the change you want to see in the world. "Everyone should have...."

Everyone should have the liberty to openly and honestly talk about sex and their sexual health no matter where they live.

Your mission: what are YOU going to do about it. "My company helps people...."

SophieBot drives open conversations on sexual health anonymously through our non-judgmental bot.

Values: Adjectives to describe your company. These are likely YOUR values. What are things you believe are a MUST HAVE for your business. Things you are very proud of your business for being.

Safe, verified, objective, reliable

Your verbal identity: how you read and sound

Firm, objective, verifiable

What kinds of things you create or do? Speeches, workshops, blog posts, etc

Podcast, talks, publish insights from questions asked

Where can you be found? Events, workplace, etc

Health hackathons, innovation weeks, safe spaces events, TedX, Healthcare symposiums

Communication channels you use most (Twitter, Instagram, groups, email, etc)

Automated Twitter, Facebook, Instagram

People/brands you associate with in public

UNFPA (United Nations Population Fund), Nailab (accelerator), Safe Spaces Kenya, Africa Healthcare Federation

About Us/Founder Origin Story

It all started with incorrect information about effective birth control. This led to an unexpected teenage pregnancy, which in turn led to an illegal abortion and a young Kenyan woman named Sophie nearly losing her life.

Irving Amukasa was in college when he heard Sophie's story, which impacted him deeply. A close friend of his, Beverly confirmed that this was indeed the case for many people she knew.

A lack of sexual health education or reliable information leads to 7.3 million unplanned births every year, and young women are especially impacted. Many abandon their dreams to care for their unplanned children. Because of societal shame, they're often shunned by their families. Most of these pregnancies could have been prevented with accurate information rather than myths and folklore related to pregnancy.

Irving devised a creative solution for this global challenge — he threw tech at the problem. He realized that talking about sex with other people was taboo in his country. But there were few social norms around talking about sex with a bot! A bot could give accurate and useful advice, safely and discreetly.

And so, came the birth of SophieBot — a friendly, geeky automated online bot that answers questions about sexual health. As people ask questions, Irving finds the answers and adds both the questions and answers to the existing SophieBot dataset.

Remember when we fixated on the "why you" earlier? This is why. In this day and age, when people have a hundred options to solve a problem, they will choose your company because of who you are. Create your origin story using the same framework as the hero's story. You've heard many of our fellow's origin stories at the start of every chapter. Now it's time to write your own.

You'll use this with everything. Your website's About Us page, your Facebook page, any media coverage. Your origin story of why you're doing this — remember we talked through the hero's story. Now it's time to tell YOUR story for why.

Prima Dona Example

Your vision: what is the change you want to see in the world? "Everyone should have…."

Clothing should not be consumed like food. It should be something that you have in your closet for decades and be something you pass on to others.

Your mission: what are YOU going to do about it? "My company helps people…."

Prima Dona offers statement clothing for AND people with a made-to-order process by Seattle designers and tailors in emerging markets.

Values: Adjectives to describe your company
Statement. Powerful. Ethical. Community.
Your verbal identity: how you read and sound
Warm. Bossy. Confident. Busy.
What kinds of things you create or do? Speeches, workshops, blog posts, etc
Create bespoke fashion
Showcase our customers on our website
Talks on building your own business as well as building strong personal brands

Where can you be found? Events, workplace, etc

Armoire events

The Riveter

Startup Events

Universities and business schools

Microsoft

Communication channels you use most (Twitter, Instagram, groups, email, etc)

Instagram

Facebook page

PrimaDonaStyle.com website

People/brands you associate with in public

The Riveter

Armoire.Style

About Us/Founder Origin Story

Since I was young, I'd associated my grandmother with being an animal loving, fiery tornado of a woman. She was the one who fed every stray dog in the neighborhood while raising four kids. But there are three words that I associate with her, above all other: The Ladies Shop. Her custom dress shop was a sanctuary for the women in her neighborhood, a place where dreams were woven.

The year was 1986, I used to sit behind the counter of the The Ladies Shop, pinning together a few scraps of fabric and trying to stay out of the way. One by one, women would come into the shop to talk to her. They would all ask for something they didn't quite have words for:

"I want something modern."

"I want something that fits well."

"I want something that no one else has."

I want something that makes me feel beautiful.

That last one was unsaid, but she knew. My grandmother always knew. Without another word, she would roll out yards and yards of silks, chiffons, cottons and voiles across the countertops. The ladies' anticipation would build with each layer of fabric until at last, a gasp of joy.

The choice was always different depending on the woman. Was it the teenager who had finally earned her freedom to make her own decision without her mother's interfering? Was it the young woman who was to be married the following week and needed an extra dosage of courage to face her in-laws? Or was it the harried mother who wanted something to cover up the scars life had ravaged upon her?

Often, it was all of these women during various phases of their life. The Ladies Shop wasn't just a place to get a new dress made. Instead it was a therapy session, a reading of a diary, a meeting with an old friend, an original safe space. Each woman's story was woven into their new dress.

"Yes, that's the one." the woman in question would reach out and caress the fabric between her fingers. "This one." The fabric was then swept away to the master tailor to create a new coat of armor to protect the woman from the modern battle she was about to fight.

At the age of six, I didn't realize what an extraordinary thing my grandmother had accomplished. She was the first woman entrepreneur I'd ever known but more than that, she was both role model and fairy godmother to women when they needed someone to look them in the eye and really understand the secret dreams they had. And doing this in the 1960s wasn't just unusual, it was unimaginable.

Now, over 30 years later, I have finally stopped wondering why I have this voice in my head that tells me that it's my mission to empower the underserved and help them achieve those secret dreams, the ones they never tell anyone. The voice in my head is my grandmother's voice. It's always been her voice commanding me to complete the mission she'd started over 50 years ago. I used to be afraid to embarking on this journey alone, but today I realize that I'm not alone. I have never been alone. She has been with me all along and she will be with me always: my muse, my role model and my fairy godmother.

A few years ago, I had the opportunity to spend time in Nigeria and Kenya, working with entrepreneurs to use technology to start and run their businesses. There, I noticed how impeccably dressed every person was—in the most colorful and unique fabrics. I designed a few original dresses for myself and some of my co-workers with these gorgeous fabrics and met some local, independent tailors to do the construction. I was very impressed at the quality of the work and the one-of-a-kind, statement nature of the final garments. These became my favorite items in my closet. They worked incredibly well for all of the aspects of my life: days in the office, being on stage at speaking engagements, and out at creative events in the evenings. Plus, they packed incredibly well for my monthly travel. I knew these were pieces that I'd keep forever—just like the pieces my grandmother used to make.

After the hundredth compliment on these dresses, I started thinking. I could provide this experience to other people as well. My vision for Prima Dona came to life. Everything would be designed in Seattle by me…but constructed in Kenya and Nigeria to provide the wonderful local tailors there the opportunity to have their work showcased at a global level.

Prima Dona has let me combine my favorite things: my family, fashion, travel, creating jobs in emerging markets and a community. When you join the Prima Dona family, you're not just adding to your closet. You're now a part of a story, a community and a powerful statement: not only are you NOT contributing to the destructive fast fashion industry, you're also ensuring a fair wage for tailors in emerging markets.

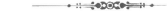

Boxes and Foxes Example

Your vision: what is the change you want to see in the world? "Everyone should have…."

No entrepreneur on the planet should be held back from starting their business because they did not attend a fancy business school or have a vast network.

Your mission: what are YOU going to do about it? "My company helps people…."

Boxes and Foxes seeks to help women and minorities solve the business challenges that are preventing them from running profitable startups

Values: Adjectives to describe your company

Scrappy, equality, hard-working, non-judgmental, creative

Your verbal identity: how you read and sound

Approachable, respectful, thoughtful, warm, we don't take ourselves too seriously

What kinds of things you create or do? Speeches, workshops, blog posts, etc

Create bespoke worksheets

Create blog posts

Conduct 1:1 consulting phone calls

Where can you be found? Events, workplace, etc

The Riveter and other co-working spaces

Startup events

Diversity and inclusion events

Communication channels you use most (Twitter, Instagram, groups, email, etc)

LinkedIn, Email, Facebook public page, Model 47 Facebook group

People/brands you associate with in public

The Riveter, Microsoft for Startups,

About Us/Founder Origin Story

You learn a lot about life from your failed startups. I worked in startups that should have worked. We had smart people with very impressive educations from Very Important Institutions. We had funding. We had office space in New York, LA and San Francisco. But we didn't have the most important thing of all: a customer.

Frustrated with my failed startup experience, I returned to New York to work in consulting. It was there that I watched 3,000 people lose their lives on 9/11/01. It was at this moment that I realized how much more I had to do with my time left on earth. I spent the next decade working in international development in emerging markets and learning about the world while volunteering in the Peace Corps in the Dominica Republic, serving as the Director of Operations for a social enterprise in Cambodia and Laos, studying climate change in Costa Rica, and then working at the United Nations in Paris leading educational software projects in Africa and Asia.

After this, I wanted to formalize my business skills, so I attended business school where I learned many frameworks and concepts. Once I started working at Microsoft, I realized so many would benefit from what I'd learned. When I created this fellowship program, little did I know that everything I'd ever done had led me there.

During the fellowship program, I realized that every entrepreneur was stuck on one specific thing. For some it was figuring out their breakeven. For others it was figuring out their technology stack. For many, it was understanding how to tell their story.

Often this one thing was the one holding them back from turning their business into a profitable business. It has been my pleasure to debug business plans and help entrepreneurs solve these problems, one-by-one.

One morning I watched my toddler daughter climb into an open moving box, her stuffed fox in tow. Much like a fox, she is scrappy, curious, and determined. Look out, world: she's a future entrepreneur for sure. I named my business for my daughter, but also for all you scrappy, curious and determined entrepreneurs. My mission is to help non-traditional entrepreneurs understand their business models and whether it's a hobby, a business or a non-profit. How can I help you?

Now it's your turn

We HIGHLY recommend you do this section with someone else. It's much easier and way more fun to talk this creative thinking through. Plus, they will be able to tell you things about your business that you might be too close to. In your workbook, please fill out the following:

- ෬ Your vision: what is the change you want to see in the world? "Everyone should have...."
- ෬ Your mission: what are YOU going to do about it? "My company helps people...."
- ෬ Values: Adjectives to describe your company. These are likely YOUR values. What are things you believe are a MUST HAVE for your business. Things you are very proud of your business for being.
- ෬ Your verbal identity: how you read and sound
- ෬ What kinds of things you create or do? Speeches, workshops, blog posts, etc
- ෬ Where can you be found? Events, workplace, etc
- ෬ Communication channels you use most (Twitter, Instagram, groups, email, etc)
- ෬ People/brands you associate with in public
- ෬ About Us/Founder Origin Story

Customer Management

Caleb Ndaka, the CEO of Comp Camp (the mobile tech skills service in Kenya), has three sets of very different customers. He has students (generally young people who do NOT pay for the service). He has Community Trainers (who set up events for kids and adults). He also has Campus Trainers (who are learning skills to they can train others). This last group pays for the service). To keep track of who he's seen and not seen as well show traction, he needs to track his customers.

He tracks them in an Excel spreadsheet with the following columns:

- Name
- Phone number
- Gender
- Age
- Level of education
- Amount received (for any payments they have made)
- Remarks

He can then easily filter and sort his customers to understand whom he has served and for what skill. He can also keep in touch with them and let them know when he's offering a new service. He also encourages them to share information about his business with their communities. This winds up being a very common way for people to request training from Comp Camp.

The same is likely true for you. You're starting to get customers. How are you going to track them, make sure they're satisfied and continue to provide them value?

Your customers (or potential customers) likely fall into one of these categories.

1. They have not heard of you. You might not know who these people are.
2. They have heard of you but not purchased. You might not know who these people are.
3. They have purchased. You know who these people are.
4. They have purchased AGAIN. You know who these people are.
5. They have referred you to others. You know who these people are.

For the last three groups, what is your customer engagement IF/THEN? This is where you walk through the workflow of what happens when someone decides to buy your product. Do they receive an email? What if they decide they want a refund?

For each one of these groups of people, we'll walk through different ways to engage them. For those who:

- Have not heard of you
- Have heard of you but don't know much about your business

You'll need to spread the word so that these people hear about you AND engage with your business. Remember that in today's crazy, busy world with so many options, potential customers need to see and hear about your business about five times before they decide to engage. The next chapter of Spread the Word addresses some ideas for how to do this.

For the next set of customers who have heard of you, you know who they are. How are you tracking them, contacting them and filing away their preferences?

Tracking Customers

A very common way that people track customers when they're first starting out is a spreadsheet like Caleb does. Another more technical solution is using a Customer Relationship Management (CRM) Tool. These are many that startups use, but one that Dona is investigating for Prima Dona is called Drip. If it works for her, she will refer it to Jeremiah for Boxes and Foxes.

Whatever tool you use, a sheet of paper, a spreadsheet or a CRM tool, you should definitely be tracking this next set of customers because they are the most likely to buy your product or refer your product to others.

At the bare minimum, you need to know:

- Name
- Contact Info
- Have they purchased
- Any interesting information
- Contacting Customers

Once you are tracking your customers, you'll need to figure out how you communicate with them? Email? Text messages? Whatever it is, make sure to keep open a two-way dialogue with these customers regularly so you can continue to serve them and they can continue to give you feedback.

The customers you ABSOLUTELY should be tracking and communicating with are:

Those who have purchased your product or service.

The first 20 customers you get are very important. They are investing in you & the story you tell, not ONLY the product. They will help build your community of customers by referring people like them to your business. Make sure to shower these customers with EXCEPTIONAL customer service so that you build loyal fans rather than just "users".

Write down what your customer engagement "if/then" looks like.

IF a customer buys your product, THEN what happens? They get a text message from you? They get an email?

IF a customer is dissatisfied with your product, THEN what happens? They get a refund? They can do an exchange?

Those who have purchased your product or service AGAIN and those who have referred you to others

These are very special customers who are advocates of yours. Think of ways you can surprise them the way you would your best friend…because they are. They are best friends of your business! Can you make special products that are only available to them? For Prima Dona, Dona is naming her clothing after her repeat customers!

These repeat customers are fans of yours so how can you be a fan of theirs? Can you support them in some way? Introduce them to anyone? Showcase their work? Get creative! (Reach out to us if you need help here—this happens to be Dona's specialty!)

Remember that your customers are your most valuable asset. Every person now has a global audience. Every event they go to or experience they have is shared with people who listen to them. Even if they aren't household names, they're deeply trusted in their communities. Anyone in the world now has the potential to spark a global movement.

People really do talk about great customer service. Make it a goal that your customer service is so good, people talk about it. Go WAY above and beyond at the beginning. You'll be surprised at how this works. Think about how you'll handle the situation is unhappy with your product or service. Will you issue a refund? Will you ask for a second chance to make it right?

For the customers who have paid for your product or service, make sure to get their feedback on the entire process. Ask if you can use their feedback in creating customer testimonials for your website or social media. People are FAR MORE likely to buy once they hear good things from others like them.

Prima Dona Example

For the first two audiences: "They have not heard of you" and "they have heard of you but not purchased", Dona is running Facebook and Instagram ads to showcase the product to these people. Shei s specifically targeting these ads to women ages 25-45 who have shown an interest in business who are English-speaking. This is exactly the audience that Ioana Tanase (the hero) falls into.

For the next three audiences of

- ଔ They have purchased. You know who these people are.
- ଔ They have purchased AGAIN. You know who these people are.
- ଔ They have referred you to others. You know who these people are

Dona has created an IF-THEN that goes like this:

- ଔ IF customer orders an item THEN they receive an email with the specifics of their order that notifies them that their order is being hand-crafted by a tailor (name is specified along with a picture) and that Dona will be in touch when it's finished.
- ଔ IF an order ships to a customer, THEN they receive an email informing them of this as well as a prompt to share their story and social media channels so Dona can showcase it on our website.
- ଔ IF it's been a week since the customer has their garment, THEN they receive another email asking if they are liking their garment and if there is anything more Dona can do.
- ଔ IF a customer orders something else after an initial purchase, THEN Dona sends them an email that informs them she wants to co-create and name a garment after them.
- ଔ IF a customer wants to return a garment, THEN Dona sends them an email to issue them a refund AND the cost of sending the garment back to her.

Boxes and Foxes Example

For the first two audiences: IF "They have not heard of you" and "they have heard of you but not purchased", THEN Jeremiah is asking his satisfied customers to refer his service to their founder friends because her know the number one place entrepreneurs get their information is from OTHER entrepreneurs. A second thing he is planning to do are many speaking engagements and hold office hours at incubators and startup workspaces. A third thing he will do is write articles about very specific entrepreneurship topics on LinkedIn and other publications to showcase his advice and business.

For the next three audiences of

- ❀ They have purchased. You know who these people are.
- ❀ They have purchased AGAIN. You know who these people are.
- ❀ They have referred you to others. You know who these people are

Jeremiah has created the following IF/THEN:

- ❀ IF the customer has filled out the initial request form with their business's information and supplies a small payment, THEN Jeremiah will send them a tailored worksheet.
- ❀ IF the customer is happy, THEN Jeremiah adds them to his newsletter where he shares exclusive advice.
- ❀ IF the worksheet is not enough, THEN Jeremiah will set up a Skype call
- ❀ For customers who have used his service for a larger fee.
- ❀ IF the customer refers another entrepreneur, THEN Jeremiah provides them another worksheet or Skype call for free as a thank you.

MODEL 47

Now it's your turn

Think about your customers in the six different categories. What's your plan for each category for Tracking, Contacting and Maintaining Preferences?

1. They have not heard of you. You might not know who these people are.
2. They have heard of you but not purchased. You might not know who these people are.
3. They have purchased. You know who these people are.
4. They have purchased AGAIN. You know who these people are.
5. They have referred you to others. You know who these people are.
6. What is your customer engagement IF/THEN for all of the above?

Spread the Word

"Does the pulling out method work?"

This was a question a 15-year-old boy asked SophieBot. Irving Amukasa promptly added the question to Sophie's dataset along with the correct answer: NO.

How did this teenage boy learn about SophieBot in the first place? Simple. Because Irving Amukasa, CEO of SophieBot, planned for him to. A few weeks earlier, Irving and his business partner Beverly had appeared on *Lion's Den*. That had done this for two reasons. They were seeking funding, of course, but they also sought to *spread the word* about their business. They followed *Lion's Den* application process. Within a week they received a note that they were going to be on the show. On recording day, they hung out at the studio from 5am, waiting for their slot to pitch. Their moment finally arrived at 4pm. Following their pitch, they received $40,000 in funding in exchange for 33% of the company.

Why do all this? Irving knew one fundamental truth. Not all social media was equal. He had to go to where his customers were consuming information to be able to advertise their services. In his case, the urban youth he was targeting were watching TV. They were interested in shows such as *Lion's Den*. So, while Irving was hustling for funding, he was ALSO getting free advertisement for his product.

For your business, you have to go where your target customers are. A great place to start is to identify the key channels through which your hero gets their information.

If it's traditional social media (Twitter, Instagram, Facebook, LinkedIn, Snapchat, etc), you need to create content that will resonate with your hero at some regular cadence. Remember, YOU are the expert on the topic you have created a business around so you need to be creating and sharing content that's related to your business…but also the industry as a whole. We highly recommend you choose 1-2 channels and focus on them extensively, rather than trying to have presence across 7 channels and doing none of them well. Figure out what kind of content make sense for your business. For long-form written content, LinkedIn, Medium and other blogging sites work well. For short-form written content, Twitter works well. For visual content, Instagram, Facebook and YouTube work well. It all depends on what represents your business best. Hit us up if you need help with this—this is Dona's favorite thing to figure out!

How can you target your company's marketing messages so your hero (and others like them—who do not yet know you) can encounter them in their daily life?

Let's explore some other channels our entrepreneurial friends have used. Kelechi and Kido of Dilish Foods (who sell back time to African families with their ready-to-eat akara beans) got creative in marketing their product. They organized side-of-the-road cooking stations to attract people on their commutes. They also hosted cooking contests with winners in categories like "Best Looking Bean Dish."

Caleb Ndaka teaches digital skills to people in mostly rural areas of East Africa. His target customers are likely not watching TV or hanging out online. He advertises by doing village-to-village tours. In each village, he befriends the main community contact, then attends locally organized gatherings such as bazaars and youth events. He puts up flyers in the central gathering place of each village. A few times, he's hired people to drive around with speakers fastened to a vehicle announcing these classes. He hosts coding and typing classes in local churches or schools.

If your customers are farmers, they likely don't hang out on Facebook all day. However, they likely DO listen to the radio. Ibrahim Aboki of Basmalah Enterprises (solar powered irrigation for farmers) participates in agricultural radio shows on the local FM channels. He also spends time building one-on-one relationships with farmers he meets through various Farmer Clubs.

Each of these entrepreneurs knows they have to showcase different content that appeals to different audiences on each individual channel. They know that as the expert on the topic, they are the best marketing tool out there. They need to constantly speak, write, mentor on this topic. They've realized their content doesn't need to be flawless, but it has to make people FEEL something. Their content has to evoke emotion (wonder, happiness, sadness, anger, outrage) and make want to share it with others. The more you can tie your business to something in your customer's lives, the more likely they are to share it with others.

An easy way to come up with ideas for content are the questions! Your content should talk directly to your users. If a customer asks a question, this is an excellent topic for you to address. Co-create this too.

Lastly, keep track of what people are saying about your product. One easy way to do this is to set a google alert for your business name or category to see what shows up in the news.

Prima Dona Example

For Prima Dona, Dona knows the most important thing she can show are the clothes and lifestyle of her customers. She's created Facebook and Instagram pages for Prima Dona. She asks each of her satisfied customers to refer three people and submit their pictures and stories for the website and social media. She is also running Instagram and Facebook ads targeted to women ages 25-45 who buy clothing online.

Both her Facebook and Instagram pages have content about her existing customer AND behind-the-scenes look into how her line is made. She is not looking into any other social media channels such as Twitter, LinkedIn, YouTube, Snapchat, etc in order to remain focused.

Boxes and Foxes Example

For Boxes and Foxes, Jeremiah is seeking to get a regular writing gig/column on a well-read website like Entrepreneur or Huffington Post. He shares stories and advice for entrepreneurs, referring to his business at the bottom of each post.

He's asking each satisfied customer to refer one other founder friend. He knows that the most common place startup founders seek advice is from other founders. He also shares general advice and ideas on his personal blog on JeremiahMarble.com, plus on LinkedIn and Twitter. He is keeping his social footprint small, focused on channels that work well with his written content.

What about you? What are your real-life channels and online channels? What is the target audience of each? What kind of content will you broadcast on each?

Help Your Customers Be Influencers

If you've done your homework properly and have been co-creating with your hero, they are likely a fan of yours and your product by now.

> Your early-adopter customers and the people who have referred you to others (from the last chapter) are ALSO some of the best marketing opportunities you have. You should be co-creating both your product AND your marketing plan with them.

We introduced you earlier to Damilola Samuel, working on Greenpad Concepts. He's using banana plant fiber, readily available in Nigeria, to produce absorbent and inexpensive sanitary napkins for rural women.

Did you know that in addition to his customers using the product, they are also acting as brand ambassadors for him? Not only do rural women who use the product produce and sell the fiber to Greenpad, but they are also employed to produce the pads and distribute them locally within their own networks. Their role as product ambassadors increases customer reach and works to eliminate the stigma and taboos surrounding menstruation. Three women currently spread the word about Greenpad Concepts: Mrs. Olatunji Janet, Mrs. Joseph Omolara and Mrs. Ojo Bose.

These women are obviously fans of the product. Not only do they create them and support their families with their salaries. They also *use* the product every month.

Why would they NOT evangelize the product? Word-of-mouth marketing is the best marketing! Who better to market your product than your best customers?

Leah creates jobs for Kenyan tailors with her modern high-quality tailoring business Mshonaji. She knows her target audience is on Instagram, Facebook and come into her coffee shop, Lava Latte. Many people drool over the pictures of her work and at the real pieces in the coffee shop. Even if her prices are out of their range, her fans refer their friends to Mshonaji and start saving to have their own piece someday. Leah says that word-of-mouth is one of the most powerful social tools she has. She focuses on doing excellent work for her customers. When others see her creations, in most cases they're already convinced by the time they decide to order garments of their own.

We strongly recommend you set up a close-knit group of customers who might not have been your initial targets to act as product advisors, ambassadors and evangelists. At Microsoft, we call them Insiders. This was the basis of the Windows Insider Program (where the two of us first started working together).

On top of giving your "Insiders" information so they can evangelize for you, you can do a few other things as well:

1. Offer more than just product — give them behind the scenes information on your business and how you work
2. Introduce them to your network to help them achieve their goals
3. Appreciate them loudly on all your channels
4. Answer their questions publicly so others with similar questions can get the answers also
5. Make long-term plans with them so they realize you are thinking of them as you plan your business.

Over the past few years while we've been running the Insider program, we've learned that in running a community — a tribe if you will — it's vital to create three things:

1. A very clear mission for what your business is trying to do — a rallying cry people can get behind (this should probably be your mission from the chapter on Branding)

2. A place where they can talk to you and amongst themselves (this can be as simple as a WhatsApp group)
3. A very clear call to action on what activity you want them to do next

Prima Dona Example

For Prima Dona, Dona encourages her customers to send her their pictures and stories (via a series of questions). She wants to showcase these on her website and social channels so they can be role models.

She also wants to create garments named after her top customers who refer others to her business.

- Who are some of your best customers you've been co-creating with?

  Ioana

  Raji

  Cynthia

- What is a very clear mission you can all agree on?

  That people need interesting, statement clothing that works for both the office and for side-hustles and speaking engagements

- How can they engage with you and each other?

  Social media and the website

- What is the call to action you will give them?

  - *Wear your Prima Dona and share pics on social media*
  - *Refer 3 people to join the tribe*

- How will you recognize their work? Featuring them on your website? Showcasing them on your social channels? Profit sharing?

  - *Featuring them on her website and her articles*
  - *Showcase them on her social channels*
  - *Heromake them in any media publications Dona's featured in*

Boxes and Foxes Example

For Boxes and Foxes, Jeremiah encourages his customers to tell their friends about his service. He uses their pictures and stories to showcase their success on his website and social channels, presenting them as examples to inspire other startup founders he hasn't yet worked with.

ଔ Who are some of your best customers you've been co-creating with?
- *Rachel and Jessica (Equilo)*
- *Ioana (starting her own business, Track and Fuel)*
- *Dona (Prima Dona)*
- *Dr. Moses Keller (SonoCare)*

ଔ What is a very clear mission you can all agree on?
   That anyone in the world should be able to access the tools and network they need to start and run a profitable business.

ଔ How can they engage with you and each other?
- *The Model 47 Facebook group to engage with each other.*
- *Email, Facebook group and LinkedIn to engage with me.*

ଔ What is the call to action you will give them?
   Chase success…and call me if you need help.

ଔ How will you recognize their work? Featuring them on your website?
- *Showcasing them on your social channels? Profit sharing?*
- *Featuring them on my website and my articles*
- *Showcase them on my social channels*
- *Heromake them in any media publications I'm featured in*

Now it's your turn!

ભ Who are some of your best customers you've been co-creating with?

ભ What is a very clear mission you can all agree on?

ભ How can they engage with you and each other?

ભ What is the call to action you will give them?

ભ How will you recognize their work? Featuring them on your website? Showcasing them on your social channels? Profit sharing?

Launch the Product

Launch Day! This is easily the most exciting and most petrifying part of this whole entrepreneurial process.

We strongly recommend a "soft-launch" with a small group of people who will give you honest feedback.

When Olayinka "Yinka" was ready to launch his e-learning for law students site Lawcademy, he didn't expect his site to crash on day one. Yinka toured many law schools all across Lagos, Nigeria, talking to students about his business — making the complex law-school concepts easy to learn. He'd gotten a great response. He was expecting about 100 people to sign up on day one. Instead, a THOUSAND did. His site was unable to handle the load. As such, he and his team had to run around and change their technology stack to handle the demand. Always be prepared for overwhelming success!

Irving Amukasa, CEO of SophieBot, (the Kenyan sexual health bot) had an adventurous product launch AND re-launch. He'd spent years building relationships with various developer groups in East Africa. He'd helped coach and mentor up and coming developers, and had shared whatever information that would be relevant for them with them. He and his friends started talking about the product while it was still in development across these different dev groups so the name SophieBot stuck in people's heads. Even though SophieBot first launched with just three questions and answers, Irving was able to hustle a TV spot after which they hit 250 users. After the TV spot, the app was thrown out of the Google Play store due to copyright issues (they had used Star Wars R2D2 beeps while the app loaded). They created a new launch sound and 70 new responses based on questions their 250 users asked. Then they re-launched on the store.

For Leah Otieno of Mshonaji fashion, her launch was much more low-key. She made garments for a group of customers who wore them out at a variety of social events. When people were asked where they got their beautiful clothing from, they all pointed at Mshonaji, gracefully and slowly spreading the message via word-of-mouth.

Is there a way you can do an event to launch your product? This gets people excited about your product and makes it "real". If you are using social media, create a hashtag for the event and ask everyone to share on social using that hashtag. For example, when we launched our fellowship, we created the #Insiders4Good hashtag. We made temporary tattoos and stickers and handed them out at our event launch. We made signs with the hashtag and encouraged everyone to share what they were doing there on social media. We were trending in both Nigeria and Kenya within the hour!

It's absolutely FINE to re-launch if you didn't get the appropriate amount of attention you were hoping for. What is that appropriate amount? Only you know that. It can be the number of people you reached or the kind of people you reached.

Another thing to think about is a re-brand. If your brand is not resonating with your core audience, think through why. Is it the price? Is it the product? Is it the service?

You don't want to keep re-launching and re-branding, so give it a few months.

The Co-Creation Hub founders, Bosun, Tunji and Femi operate on the belief that you'll know if you have a business in six months. It's much too difficult to tell before then — so be patient!

Last and MOST important you might not have a insanely huge launch success. Often people who do have these HUGE launches have trouble with scale and have to reset customer expectations, tarnishing their brand. Focus on getting customers, one after another. With each customer's feedback, your product will get better. You'll build one fan after another and ensure you can scale to meet their needs.

Prima Dona Example

- What is your launch plan? Are you doing a soft-launch or a broad-launch?
  Soft-launch
- Will you have a physical event?
  Yes, a party at her house featuring fashion by Armoire and Prima Dona
- Will you have media attention lined up?
  Not until she has 10 customers.
- Will you have a place online to direct people to?
  Her website
- How will you handle the large amount of attention your product may generate?
  Communicate about our process with our customers via emails
- How will you know if your launch is successful? What are the triggers that will tell you that you need a re-launch and/or a re-brand?
  She'll know her launch is successful if she has 10 customers who love her product, are showcased on her website and are willing to talk about it to others.

Boxes and Foxes Example

- What is your launch plan? Are you doing a soft-launch or a broad-launch?
  Soft-launch

- Will you have a physical event?

    Office hours at The Riveter

- Will you have media attention lined up?

    Not until I help 10 customers solve the problem they approached him with

- Will you have a place online to direct people to?

    - *His website*

    - *The Model 47 Facebook group*

- How will you handle the large amount of attention your product may generate?

    - *Take on projects that are high-impact to society.*

    - *Be willing to say no to opportunities.*

- How will you know if your launch is successful? What are the triggers that will tell you that you need a re-launch and/or a re-brand?

    He'll know his launch is successful if he has 10 customers in the first three months who he has helped solve business challenges for

Now it's your turn!

- What is your launch plan? Are you doing a soft-launch or a broad-launch?
- Will you have a physical event?
- Will you have media attention lined up?
- Will you have a place online to direct people to?
- How will you handle the large amount of attention your product may generate?
- How will you know if your launch is successful? What are the triggers that will tell you that you need a re-launch and/or a re-brand?

Seek Investment Cautiously

Recently, a founder friend from Latin America wrote to us. Dr. María had received an offer for funding and wondered whether to take it. Her question was like others we've gotten, so we asked her if we could share our process for answering it. She gave us permission, if we kept her identity anonymous and didn't reveal personal details. ("Dr. María" is not her real name.)

An investor had offered Dr. María $150,000 in order to scale her operations to new regions of her country. (She was conducting mobile EKG tests for people living in rural areas). There were several parts to the offer, but the most important part was the condition for a "5% revenue share" for five years. After five years, the financing would be considered repaid. The question she needed to answer was: should she take the $150,000? If she did, for every $1.00 of revenue she brought in over the next five years, she'd need to give her investor $0.05.

To answer her question, we started with a breakeven for Dr. María. For each EKG test, she charged a price of $8. We needed to find out how much of that price (revenue) was profit. She told us that she was currently paying a unit cost of $3.2 *for each test* to local agents in "finders fees." We thought this to be expensive, but Dr. María explained that there was a good deal of corruption in her city, so for political reasons she needed to pay those kickbacks. Those fees were her only variable costs.

Assuming that for now Dr. María couldn't avoid paying the finders fees, we then wanted to determine how much profit Dr. María made per EKG test. (As you remember, her profit per test was her *price per test* minus her *unit cost per test*). We calculated that $8 - $3.2 = $4.80 profit per test, after referrer fees.

Next, we needed to find out what Dr. María paid each month. She added up her monthly costs (salaries, marketing, car payments plus gas, phone, supplies, utilities), and told us that she was paying $2,730 in monthly fixed costs. Although we could have treated supplies as part of her variable price, we left them for simplicity.

Dr. María needed to pay those monthly costs with the profit from the tests she administered. If she sold zero tests in a month, she would lose a full $2,730 that month.

We needed to figure out how many tests she needed to sell, in order to break even and raise at least $2,730 in profit.

So, we had this equation: $2,730 = number of tests x $4.80 profit per test

Simplifying, we had: number of tests a month = $2,730 / $4.80

number of tests a month = 569 tests

Doing that division told that us that Dr. María needed to sell 569 tests every month (right now) in order to cover her monthly fees: 569 x $4.80 = $2,731.2. (If she sold 569 tests in a month, she would *make* $1.20 in profit above her monthly costs of $2,730.)

Now that we knew Dr. María *needed to sell* 569 EKGs per month to break even, we wanted to see how many tests she *actually sold*. She told us she was selling about 18 tests daily, and that she worked Monday through Saturday (so was open for business 6 days a week). This gave us the following equation:

18 tests a day, x 6 days a week, x 4.3 weeks a month = 464 tests a month

The above equation let us know that we had a problem. According to those numbers, even before taking the investment, Dr. María was only selling 464 tests a month, but her break-even was 569 tests a month.

464 x $4.80 profit per test = $2,229 profit per month

monthly profit ($2,229) - monthly costs ($2,730) = -$501

If those numbers were right, she was *losing $501 every month!*

At this point, though, Dr. María let us know that she "had been working alone recently." She told us that, when she works with another doctor to administer EKG tests, she can see up to 32 patients daily (double the rate of patients she can see by herself). However, the previous doctor had moved away six months ago. That other doctor taken along with him his $1,000/month salary. Dr. María had made an error in her original calculation. She had estimated her monthly fees as *if the other doctor were still working.* That meant that the monthly fixed costs were $1,000 too high.

We needed to recalculate our breakeven. Subtracting out the other doctor's salary, we took $2,730 - $1,000 to get her revised monthly fixed costs of $1,730. Her "profit per test" remained the same: $4.80 per test.

Now we had this: $1,730 = number of tests x $4.80 profit per test

Simplifying, we had: number of tests = $1,730 / $4.80

number of tests = 361 tests a month

So the revised breakeven was $1,730 / $4.80, or 361 tests per month to break even. (361 x $4.80 = $1,732.8, so she'd make 80 cents if she sold at least 361.)

According to our earlier calculation, we knew Dr. María sold 18 tests a day, x 6 days a week, x 4.3 weeks a month, or about 464 tests each month. She was making profit using these new calculations: 464 - 361 = 103 tests OVER breakeven each month.

464 x $4.80 profit per test = $2,229 profit per month

monthly profit ($2,229) - monthly costs ($1,730) = $499

Using the revised estimates for her monthly costs, she was *making $499 every month. (Much better!)*

Now we needed to remember the question we were originally trying to answer: should Dr. María take the $150,000 investment or not?

She was charging a price of $8 per test, which is her revenue per test. If she needed to share 5% of that revenue, that would be $8 x .05, or $.40 per test to be shared with investors. Even before the rev share, she was already paying $3.2 to referrers. She would need to add to her unit costs the price she'd need to pay to her potential investor under the terms of the rev share ($0.40) per test

> new profit per test = price − referrer fee − rev share with investor
> new profit per test = $8.00 − $3.20 − $0.40
> new profit per test = $4.40

If she took the rev share investment, Dr. María would make $4.40 per test in profit ($0.40 less profit per test than before).

If Dr. María took the investment, she'd still have the same monthly costs of $1,730. Her new profit per test (at 5% of revenue) would be $4.40, so her new breakeven each month would be $1,730 / $4.40 = 394 tests per month to make a profit. Remember, Dr. María sold 18 tests a day, x 6 days a week, x 4.3 weeks a month = 464 test sold each month, so 464 - 394 = 70 tests over breakeven.

> 464 x $4.40 profit per test = $2,041.6 profit per month
> monthly profit ($2,041.6) - monthly costs ($1,730) = $311.6

Even if she took the investment, and sold zero additional tests, she would be able to pay her monthly costs. Moreover, if she took the $150,000 investment, Dr. María would be able to purchase additional equipment, and potentially hire an additional doctor, which would increase the number of tests she could sell each month.

Our advice to Dr. María, therefore, was that she accept the investment terms.

EXAMPLE BREAK-EVEN

MONTHLY FIXED COSTS

SALARIES	$~~$2,030~~ $1,030
MARKETING (RADIO, ETC)	$ 50
VEHICLE + GAS	$ 237
PHONE	$ 156
SUPPLIES	$ 157
UTILITIES	$ 100
	$~~2,730~~ $1,730

PRICE: $8 PER TEST   (x5% = $.40)

COST PER UNIT	PROFIT PER UNIT
NOW: $3.20	→ $8 - $3.20 = $4.80
@5%: $3.2 + $.4 = $3.6	→ $8 - $3.60 = $4.40

BREAK-EVEN

NOW: ~~$2,730~~ / $4.80 = ~~569~~ TESTS PER MONTH
$1,730 / $4.80 = $\boxed{361}$ "   "   "

@5%: ~~$2,730~~ / $4.40 = ~~621~~ TESTS PER MONTH
$1,730 / $4.40 = $\boxed{394}$ "   "   "

CURRENT # TESTS

18 TESTS / DAY × 6 DAYS / WEEK × 4.3 WEEKS / MONTHS =
$\boxed{464}$ TESTS PER MONTH

One of our fundamental beliefs is that you should seek additional funding only when you can't keep up with demand. We encourage all our founders to aim for profitability and to scale through customer revenue. We believe that too much reliance on outside funding can hide the profitability of your core business (which can make it difficult for you if investment dries up later on), and also too frequently requires that you give up flexibility (in the form of ownership and/or cash flow) to your investors. More practically, for many of the non-traditional founders we work with, gaining access to funding—whether from angel investors, VCs, or even small business loans at a reasonable interest rate—can be tough.

However, we acknowledge that reality is usually a bit more complex. Each entrepreneur has a different vision of what scale looks like. For some founders, "getting to scale" entails selling 10% more units each month than they currently do. Some won't be happy until they double their current sales. Others won't rest until they sell exponentially more than they do currently.

Entrepreneurs seeking exponential growth — and even those trying to sell enough units to pay for a large purchase (such as a big piece of equipment or a factory or an expanded salesforce, for example) — find that they need to seek outside investment. They simply can't fund the scale they seek from their own pockets or from friends.

Moreover, funding can take a while to track down. Successful entrepreneurs looking to scale (scale their production, their marketing, their tech infrastructure, etc.) will need to forecast future sales based on realistic estimates of *having scaled*. If you build a new factory, you'll be able to produce WAY more than you currently do—which will affect every other part of the business, potentially including your price. You'll need to pursue investment well in advance of the additional sales they desire.

If this describes you, there are several options available to you. At this stage of your business, you may not yet have a good idea of what your exit strategy will be, down the road. However, keeping an eye on your finances is something that you will need continuously to keep in mind. You probably won't know which option is best (or even which options are *available* to you) until you've established scale and a position in the market with a clear growth trajectory.

Going too deep into investment options is beyond the scope of this book, and likely not yet super useful for you. However, there are a few things that you'll want to keep in mind. It's also useful to have a framework for how to think about investment. We'd like to share these with you here.

Raising money (investment) in the form of...

Customer revenue

In the "Calculate Your Break-Even" section earlier, we described the equation to answer the question "During this month, how many units do I have to sell, in order NOT TO LOSE MONEY?"

(Number of Units to Break Even) = (Monthly Fixed Costs) / (Profit per Unit)

You may have noticed that, to figure out the profitability of our business each month, we used ALMOST all the variables in our worksheet. To calculate break even, we need our unit of sale, our monthly fixed costs, our costs per unit of sale, and our average evenue per sale (often our price). Catch one variable we DIDN'T mention?

That's right! We didn't consider our "investment fixed costs." Remember, the investment fixed costs are the costs you incur before you begin, which you want to pay off at some point. Of course, these costs are related to other parts of your break-even equation. (For example, buying a factory or investing in better equipment can reduce your "costs per unit." Paying for a big marketing investment will (hopefully) increase the number of units you sell.) However, the relationship between these investments and your break-even equation is indirect.

First, however, you need to *do* your breakeven equation. Knowing your profit per unit can help you think about your investment costs in terms of its worth in sales. For example, how many cups of coffee do you need to sell, to pay off your espresso machine?

As an example, let's look again at Origin Stories Coffee to see how this might work.

Scaling through customer revenue: Origin Stories Coffee

To understand how Origin Stories Coffee could scale through customer revenue, we only need to know three types of information (all of which we first saw in earlier chapters): its sales unit, its profit per sales unit, and the table of investment costs.

Here is that information for Origin Stories:

Sales Unit: Cup of Coffee

Profit per Sales Unit: $3.50

Investment Costs:

Description	Unit	Cost Per Unit	# Units	Subtotal
A cool sign for outside	One sign	$100	1	$100
Price list sign	One sign	$25	1	$25
Tables	Per table	$5,000	10	$5,000
Chairs	Per chair	$100	20	$2,000
Espresso maker	One machine	$10,000	1	$10,000
Mugs	Pack of 10	$50	4	$200
Blankets	Pack of 5	$100	4	$400
Sound system	One item	$1,000	1	$1,000
Refrigerator	One item	$1,000	1	$1,000
Dishwasher	One item	$1,000	1	$1,000
TOTAL INV				**$20,725**

Notice for the table of investment costs, we just copied the table directly from earlier in the book. To restate each of the investment line items, we simply divide that line's subtotal by the profit per unit. For example, to figure out how many cups of coffee we'd need to sell *above and beyond breakeven* to pay off the "cool sign for outside," we merely divide its cost ($100) by our profit per unit ($3.50)—which is 29 cups of coffee (rounding up from 28.5).

Description	Unit	Cost Per Unit	# Units	Subtotal	# cups of coffee
A cool sign for outside	One sign	$100	1	$100	29
Price list sign	One sign	$25	1	$25	8
Tables	Per table	$5,000	10	$5,000	1,428
Chairs	Per chair	$100	20	$2,000	572
Espresso maker	One machine	$10,000	1	$10,000	2,858
Mugs	Pack of 10	$50	4	$200	58
Blankets	Pack of 5	$100	4	$400	115
Sound system	One item	$1,000	1	$1,000	286
Refrigerator	One item	$1,000	1	$1,000	286
Dishwasher	One item	$1,000	1	$1,000	286
TOTAL INV				**$20,725**	**5,922**

This equation helps us estimate how long we'd need to "self-fund" from our sales, in order to pay off the investment. We'd use this equation:

[number of months to repay investment] =

(investment) / [(# forecast sales a month) – (breakeven sales a month)]

First, we need to figure out what our monthly sales forecast looks like:

We estimate that we'll sell *50 cups of coffee a day*, on average

We're open *6 days a week*

There are *30 days in the average month*

Forecast monthly sales = (units sold per day) x (days open) x (days a month)

Forecast monthly sales = (50) x (6) x (30)

Forecast monthly sales = 9,000

Now that we have our forecast for monthly sales, we can estimate how long we'd need to "self-fund" from our sales, in order to pay off the investment. We'd use this equation:

[number of months to repay investment] =

(investment) / [(# forecast sales a month) – (breakeven sales a month)]

number of months to repay investment = 5,922 / [(9,000 – 5,800)]

number of months to repay investment = 5,922 / 3,200

number of months to repay investment = 1.85 months

So—if all of our assumptions are right, we would be able to pay off our initial investments within the first two months.

In M47, we've focused primarily on helping you understand, plan, launch, and sustain your business, growing it with customer revenue based on a solid, profitable business model. Going too deep into investment models is beyond the scope of this book, but we thought we'd give you a few examples of investment we've seen founders use.

We've ordered them roughly along their attractiveness to the typical startup. Of course, every startup is different and every specific investment opportunity is unique (PLEASE read the fine print before signing anything) – but types of investment in general fall into patterns.

Raising money (investment) in the form of...

A grant

A grant is essentially "free money" given to organizations that are working on behalf of (usually) a social issue. Often, there aren't onerous restrictions on how the funds are spent. (Jeremiah once worked at an organization whose CEO said "once we win the grant, we'll do what's right for the business, not EXACTLY what we wrote down in the grant application.") Usually, grants pay out funds in "tranches:" certain requirements or milestones must be met before further funds will be paid out.

For example, some governments (local, state, and national) offer grants to social businesses and NGOs working to address substance abuse or homelessness. There are also UN bodies or international foundations and NGOs that themselves offer grants to organizations working in certain fields of interest (including infectious disease, poverty-reduction, and gender equality).

In general, this is the absolute best type of investment type for founders, but they're few and far in between. Most startups don't qualify (many of these grants specify that they can only be awarded to NGOs or non-profit organizations).

At the time of this writing, Dr. Moses of SonoCare is applying for several grants in the area of maternal health, and Rachel of Equillo is waiting to hear the results of their own grant applications. Good luck, both!

Crowdfunding

Caleb Ndaka of Comp Camp used the crowdfunding model to to raise money for laptops, projectors and a van. He was trying to raise funds to buy 20 additional laptops at $300 each, two additional projectors for use in his classrooms, as well as a van. With his aim to reach rural communities, he sought a more reliable means of transportation to move devices and trainers efficiently and effectively. He estimated that purchasing a van in Nairobi would cost around $25,000. He started a crowdfunding campaign on Kickstarter to raise that amount.

Side hustle as income

In the final days of her life, the only thing Yinka's mother could keep down was fresh juice with no preservatives or added sugar. Yinka decided to start a side hustle of bottling this juice to help others. He used the profits to fund his main business Lawcademy.ng, (an e-learning platform he created for Nigerian law students, now used by over 2,200 Nigerian law schools students).

In most of the developing world, VC or angel investment opportunities are near 0%, so Yinka and our other 45 entrepreneurs have to be endlessly creative to keep their businesses running. We're incredibly honored to learn from them every day.

Revenue Share

The story of Dr. María at the beginning of this chapter is a common example of "rev share." An investor is willing put invest a certain amount of money into your business, in exchange for a percentage of your revenue. The timing by which you repay this investment varies, but usually it's monthly or quarterly, or sometimes after your business has met certain milestones.

There are a number of benefits to the startup founder of this form of investment. One big one is that the time frame of repayment is usually limited (for example to three or five years), and also you're not typically asked to trade away too much of the future growth of your business (as you'd do through equity). The easiest way to assess whether you should take the money is by adding the investor's cut to your costs per unit, as we demonstrated above.

Debt / Loan

Although it can be difficult for startup founders—especially early in the lifespan of their businesses—to approach a bank for funding, it is possible. Typically, a bank or other lender would offer financing in return for a guaranteed repayment each month. That repayment consists of interest (the incentive for the lender to offer you money) as well as principal (repaying the actual money borrowed). Frequently a lender would seek "collateral" for such a loan, including the business's assets (like tables, chairs, and an expresso machine in the case of Origin Stories Coffee) or even other assets (like the founder's home mortgage or car).

This sort of investment arrangement with new, unproven businesses can be risky to lenders, and so they protect themselves against this risk of failure by charging higher interest rates. One of the difficulties to founders is that lenders require a regular repayment of principal and interest each month—which ends up being part of the monthly fixed costs and included as part of the break-even.

Equity

The most publicized form of startup financing is equity from investors like venture capital (VC) firms and "angel investors." Venture capital financing is well beyond the scope of this book, but we encourage you to get some solid advice before seeking to go this route!

ACT IV

Progress Tracking

You did it! How do you feel? Thrilled? Petrified? Exhausted? GOOD! That means you're doing it right. By now you've likely realized that you're never actually done. You likely need to go back over some sections, make adjustments, do another test, reduce a variable, add back in a variable and so much more.

You're doing great. To help you track and measure your progress, this section is full of handy tools that we have used over and over again.

Measure Your Success

Remember last time you did something perfectly on the FIRST try? Exactly.

Doesn't happen that often, does it?

We've learned that for most people, your first idea is often not your best one. If your business has gained no traction in six months, it might be time to change a variable. Don't beat yourself up, but rather be kind to yourself for having gotten this far; for having had the courage to start in the first place. A while ago, you had no clue about starting a business. Now you know exactly what TO do and what to NOT do.

John Mugendi started his entrepreneurial journey by attempting to create a breast cancer detection system. He was not getting many customers — women didn't find him to be reliable. What they DID like was the community John set up — On Fleek, a virtual "hospital waiting room" where women who've been diagnosed with breast cancer can discuss the deeply vulnerable topics they felt uncomfortable talking about with anyone else. In his case, his initial solution wasn't the right fit for the problem these women faced, BUT he was able to pivot and find a problem that he knew how to solve.

Let's debug and figure out exactly what is not working for your business. For each of the questions below, HONESTLY answer: Yes, No, or I don't know.

It's OKAY if you don't know — this gives you a path to where you should investigate further.

Question	Honest Answer	What you're going to do next
Are you the right person to tackle this idea? *(Do you have passion, skills, network, and expertise, or can you get them?)*		
Have you chosen the right hero? *(Are you building for the right person?)*		
Does your hero agree? *(That the problem you're trying to solve is a real one for them?)*		
Is your solution the right one for the problem?		
Is your idea better than competition or alternates?		
Have you listed all the assumptions you can think of?		
Have you tested all your assumptions?		
Do you have a prototype that is viable enough for your hero to test?		
Do you have a co-create loop to get immediate feedback from your hero?		
Have you done the math? Does the math tell you that you ave a viable business?		
Have you hustled the right people to help?		
Are you telling the hero's story in a compelling way?		
Are your customers acting as influencers?		
Do you have the right visibility with your target customers through good marketing and branding?		
Do you have the money you need to grow further?		

#TextableTribe

There are going to be hard days. Lots of them. There are also going to be a ton of wonderful days. For both of these kinds of days, we've found it's vital to have people you can call or text or visit who will reassure you or celebrate with you. Likely the people who will reassure you and advise you are diferent than those who will celebrate wtih you. No matter who it is, these are people who are on your side. We call them our #TextableTribe. Who is your texable tribe? What specially will you call on each person for. We've added ourselves to your #TextableTribe.

Person	I will contact them if
Jeremiah and/ or Dona	I need help with a business problem I need someone to tell me I'm not crazy

Other People to Contact

You will also discover there are people you need to contact for reasons other than support. You might have a specific question. You might need a favor. These are people who you will likely have more transactional relationships with. Who are they?

Person	I will contact them for

Things to Follow-Up On

As you go along, you'll find a ton of things that you don't yet know the answer to or need to investigate more. We like to have one place to track them and put a due date by which to address them to keep ourselves on track. What are yours?

Item	Get an answer by...

Pro/Cons

You're going to be conflicted on many things as you start and run this business. One tool we have used over and over again is the Pro/Con list. It's fairly simple but incredibly helpful. We like to do this with others to help broaden our thinking. Simply write down the Pros and Cons of any decision you are struggling with, whether it's something as simple as color of your logo or something as complex as whether you should be in the business you're in or not.

Decision	Pros	Cons

Epilogue: The M47 Community

The woman in the sequined top waited for a gap in traffic, then dashed across the four-lane road. She moved with the ease of someone who did this frequently. She ducked behind the overflowing bus. Darted in front of the impatient, sputtering motorbike. Sauntered—head held high—past the pickup truck loaded with eight young men. (Of course, they all swung round excitedly to watch her.) Her dance seemed well-practiced; her partner, the daily traffic. At last with a flourish, she flung open a door and disappeared into a brown-roofed hut.

Most roofs were brown in Ibadan, Nigeria. The beating rains had long ago rusted their corrugated iron from its gleam and shimmer. Faded it. Crusted it. The Ibadan roofs had adapted to their surroundings as had the city's inhabitants. We'd come to see these roofs, these people. In a sense it had all begun here in Ibadan.

In a rickety bus the two of us and our crew made the 120 km journey from Lagos to Ibadan to see the storied city. It took us three hours to drive there. Returning to Lagos took five: an overloaded tractor trailer had split in half from the weight of its cargo, blocking both lanes. We'd had to wait our turn in the darkness before our van could slog slowly through the mud beside the wreckage.

During that five-hour journey back to Lagos, we'd penned the first chapters of this book. As we wrote, the excited chatter of our crew faded dimly into the background. We'd started off writing in a small leather notebook. (One of us always carries one in case of inspiration emergencies.) We graduated to napkins and scraps of paper once we ran out of notebook pages.

Neither of us realized in that moment that we were writing the Model 47 origin story. After all, everything we'd done our whole lives had led us to Ibadan.

For about a year we'd referenced the city of Ibadan in nearly every speech we'd given as we'd talked about our #Insiders4Good program. Our friend, mentor, sponsor and spokesperson, Bambo Sofola had grown up there, son of a sociologist and one of Africa's first female playwrights. Time after time, as we described our goals for running a global entrepreneur fellowship, a program we'd invented in Bambo's office one late July afternoon, Ibadan had played a starring role.

Since that late summer day in 2016, we've spoken about our program on stages in New York and Nairobi, Los Angeles and Lagos, Seattle and St. Louis and we'd continually used Ibadan as our foundation point. From the earliest planning stage, a million miles away in Seattle, Washington, we knew that Bambo would need at some point to stand on some stage in a suit, talk about the mission of the program and recall the city of his earliest and fondest memories.

We knew this framework would need to work in Ibadan for someone like the confident woman in the sequined top. If we would really be able to live out our mission to empower every entrepreneur on the planet with the tools and skills they'd need to achieve economic opportunity, our framework would also need to work there, in the raucous, crowded city of Ibadan. So, of course, we needed to make the pilgrimage there so we could understand.

We do get it, you know. We do know that ours is a big, lofty goal. We're trying to empower every single entrepreneur on the planet. Who do we think we are? We hear you. We know that our goal will be difficult to achieve. We know that we're aiming high. But we also aren't deterred by its difficulty. We believe it's an important goal. So as we wrote this little book we kept in mind the entrepreneurs of Ibadan. We wrote it for them. And we also wrote the book for you.

We believe that through the hardest and darkest days, you can and WILL fight your way through. We know this because we have seen it over and over again.

People continually tell us things like this:

> *I didn't get accepted into (and then drop out of) Stanford*
> *I wasn't accepted into Y Combinator.*
> *I didn't work for three years at Google or Facebook or Microsoft.*

I have this great idea I know will help people, but it's super early—and I simply don't know where to start.

I don't have the right network to leverage even to ask the questions.

...so how can I build my business?

The answer is not easy, but it is simple. Network. One of the most powerful tools we've both used along our ways, called upon in moments of need—has been the networks of friends, colleagues, and former classmates we've met along the way and carefully cultivated. "Ask an expert first" has been our mantra. Asking a real, live human—better, a friend who wants to see you succeed—has been one of our crafty tricks to springboard our careers. The power of the network is forceful indeed.

After our East Africa fellowship, we had a graduation event where our entrepreneurs had a chance to pitch their businesses to an audience that included potential customers, partners, investors and media. It feels fitting to share with you the commencement speech we made, given all we've been through together for the last 270-ish pages.

What a day it's been. Scratch that. What a RIDE it's been.

We don't know about you, but we clearly remember last June when we all met. We walked into a room and there were a group of people avoiding eye contact. ESPECIALLY US. No one felt particularly confident in what they were doing there. You all had ideas of businesses you wanted to run. We had ideas of information that might help you.

Together, we stumbled through lessons of acquiring customers, MVPs, tech, and of course the infamous battle of #TeamMath vs #TeamHustle (#TeamHustle wins every time — just saying).

Sketches of business plans appeared on sticky notes.

At the end of the week, a group of trembling would-be entrepreneurs presented their visions.

Six months have passed. We have been in contact with each other every day, all hours of the day. I don't think any of us expected the relationship that has formed between all of the people in this room to have happened. We are no longer simply colleagues, we are FAMILY.

Today there were no trembling would-be entrepreneurs presenting their ideas. Today there were only confident business owners presenting their TRACTION.

We have been around the world meeting people and telling them about you. We have shared your stories at the top business schools in the world as well as entrepreneur conferences such as Websummit, Startup Grind and many other global stages. People around the world are floored at the work you are doing. We are floored at how much further along you are than ANY OTHER pitch we have heard all year.

Fellows, it's been incredible to see the amazing progress you have made. This is only the beginning of the journey as you grow these seedling businesses into powerful forests. What you have embarked upon is hard. Eradicating decades old problems is no simple task… otherwise somebody would have done it by now. We have all the faith in the world that you'll achieve your goals and so much more than any of us can imagine.

Everyone else: by being here today and supporting the fellows, you're not just making an impact on these amazing entrepreneurs. You're now a part of their Origin Story. You're making an impact in all the lives they will change because of their hard work. And that impact is exponential in this community. We hope everyone will join us in supporting the fellows as they continue to grow their businesses to empower East Africa, the continent and then, yes, every person and organization on the planet to achieve more.

Thank you.

That last bit, the part about community is the most important part of this whole book. Every entrepreneur in every country in the world agrees on this one thing. You wake up terrified at night. You constantly wonder if you're doing the right thing; wondering if it wouldn't be easier just to get a normal job.

Yes, entrepreneurship is a lonely and scary journey; but by having a community of friends and like-minded people surrounding you, we hope it's slightly less so.

As the two of us have started our own businesses, we have called on our 46 entrepreneurs almost every day. We love watching them call on each other. We love when they point to interesting opportunities that will help the others, just like the other day when Irving pointed out an interesting fashion-tech event to Leah.

We love realizing none of us are going through this alone. To fulfill our mission of helping 1000 non-traditional entrepreneurs make a profit every year, we need to all work together.

This is true for you too. You are not alone. It's vitally important that you have a community of people you can talk to on "those" days.

So, our last question (so many questions in this book, we know!) is the most important one:

Who are you going to call/message/see on the hardest days? Tell them this is going to happen. Make sure they are signed up to be there for you.

You should count on the two of us to be on that list. We want YOU to be one of our 1000 successful entrepreneurs this year. Seriously if there are topics that you don't feel are covered in enough depth or ones that are straight up missing, let us know! We're actively working on the second iteration of this book now and we'd love your feedback and story.

We hope that like our global entrepreneurs, you too will join our community and share your adventures: http://Facebook.com/groups/model47

Please keep in mind that by joining the Model 47 movement, you are now a part of a global community of people who are starting and running profitable businesses. You are never alone.

We can't wait to hear from you.

Love always,

Jeremiah and Dona

ACKNOWLEDGEMENTS AND DEDICATIONS

⬥

We owe so much to so many.

We dedicate Model 47 to our families. Jeremiah's beautiful. brilliant wife Mireya Almazán and their incredible daughter, Luciana, are Jeremiah's everything. They inspire him and propel him; they keep him from doing truly dumb things. He loves them tremendously. He thanks them for putting up with the days away traveling, and the early mornings and late nights working.

Doug Watkins is the love of Dona's life—he has been since they met (fighting over interview candidates in Mexico!) He's the reason Dona has so many jobs and adventures. He's a constant source of strength and wisdom; not only for pushing her to be better, but for his undying love and support for all of her schemes and shenanigans.

To team Nigeria, you looked at a crazy idea scribbled on a whiteboard and put your reputations on the line to make it happen. Bambo Sofola, Raji Rajagopalan, Nikki Rubino Guillermo Rueda, Fernando Sanchez Gonzalez, LaSean Smith, Thomas Trombley, Shina Oyetosho, Kendra Nnachi, Paula Wigwe — none of this, and we mean NONE OF THIS, would be possible without every single one of you. Thank you for being our #TextableTribe.

To our friends at the Co-Creation Hub in Lagos, Nigeria (especially Femi Longe, Bosun Tijani, and Tunji Eleso), thank you for your hospitality and everything you taught us. To this day, we yell the lessons we learned from you all. "YOU DON'T NEED A WEBSITE…yet."

To the folks at GrowthAfrica and The Kajiji in Nairobi, thank you for hosting us, teaching us and caring for our fellows

241

To Ioana Tanase and Blair Glennon, who had to experience 9,000 messages at weird hours because we were FINALLY done with the math section. This time for SURE. No really. Actually…we forgot a table. Dona is going to KILL Jeremiah.

To Ileana Hernandez aka Illy for the beautiful "illystrations" (because we sure as heck did not do them and they are AMAZING.)

To Dave Wright for the DETAILED re-frogging and your PASSIONATE advocacy for building for MANY and NOT A HERO. PS: We want to be invited to your parties. Don't say we KANT.

To our editor, Moleta Tumi Tladi: thank you for not thinking we're (totally) insane and the SO MANY revisions. You get it.

Thank you to Dan Holodak for creating us author pictures that doesn't make *one of us* look like a murderer. We love them!

Thank you IE, ESADE, IESE, INSEAD, LBS, Said, and Wharton for letting us infiltrate your classrooms and disrupt your students with our message. You're creating amazing generations of leaders.

To our entrepreneurs, some of whose stories we told in this book, but all of whose spirit, grit, and fun make this entire initiative real. Thank you for being our team. Thank you for answering our very random questions at very random hours. You have no idea what it means to have you as our #TextableTribe.

To the Nigerian #Insiders4Good Fellows:
To Daniel Isijola, hand-drawing Nollywood films into comic books.

To Paula Aliu, who responded to her friend's suicide by founding a service connecting people with professional mental health counseling.

To Damilola Samuel, trying to help rural girls stay in school by providing them with disposable sanitary pads made from local agricultural by-products like banana fronds.

To Ikechukwu Chukwu, helping students find affordable housing.

To Muhammad Abdullahi, letting people recycle instead of paying for trash disposal.

To Ibrahim Mohammed Aboki, who's using solar panels instead of fossil fuels to irrigate farmers' fields.

Ubio Obu, delivering hydroponic fresh fruits and vegetables to urbanites who want fresh, high-quality produce.

To Obinna Onyekwere, who's creating an online fashion platform.

To Yeshua Russel, who's powering hospitals, schools, and other essential community spaces with solar panels.

To Mubarak Adeyemo, who's helping Nigerians protect their valuables with GPS property tracking.

To Ifeoma Degge, who's providing Nigerian fashion designers better variety and prices for locally-designed fabrics.

To Kelechi Odoemena, who's making meal prep with cowpeas faster, easier, and healthier.

To Idowu Bamido, who's helping microbusinesses expand into new markets by creating them an online presence.

To Olayinka Olanrewaju, who's making studying Nigerian law simpler and more fun.

To Alexander Bamidele, who's improving academic performance through a safe platform for feedback on teachers.

To Opeyemi Paul Adekunle, who's helping Nigerian students study better for the Jamb CBT university entrance exam, and other tests.

To Ugochukwu Stephen Ugwudi, who's reducing cost and increasing the nutritional value of poultry and livestock by leveraging nutrient-rich cassava peels instead of corn.

To Dr. Moses Owoicho Enokela, who's providing convenient, affordable, and accurate health testing to the rural poor with mobile diagnostic medical imaging services.

To Ayodeji Adewusi who's validating job applicants' qualifications better and faster, through a platform that checks graduation certificates in real time.

To Omasirichukwu Udeinya who's making electronic healthcare record-keeping better and cheaper.

To Oluwaloni Olowookere reducing costs from food wastage.

To Bem Asen who's connecting retired people with jobs, internships, loans and grants.

To Johnson Bewaji, who's eliminating manual record keeping and makes business data cheaper to access real-time for Nigerian SMBs.

To Kayode Adedayo introducing tourists to Nigeria's amazing attractions and culture.

To Miracle Samuel who's helping rural Nigerians recharge their devices with automated, reliable, round-the-clock service.

To the East African #Insiders4Good Fellows:
To Alfred Ongere who's helping refugees gain access to reliable information for their surviving and thriving.

To Ange Uwambajimana , who's preventing embolisms in IV tubes through an automated IOT solution

To Brendah Nantongo, who is helping women learn to be healthy during their pregnancy.

To Caleb Ndaka, who is teaching tech education to kids AND the adults who love them.

To Collince Osewe, who is creating a trustworthy platform to administer and track vaccinations.

To Edgar Mwampinge, who is creating the AirBnB of workspaces in Kenya so anyone can start their business in an affordable space.

To Festus Okumu, founder of a mobile-based marketplace offering quick access to credit at competitive rates.

To Irving Amukasa, who is helping share trustworthy information about sexual health with East African youth.

To Job Ndiango, who is offering users a credit score using mobile money history to establish credit worthiness.

To John Mugendi who is creating a safe space for survivors of breast cancer.

To Leah Otieno who is matching people who want unique fashion with talented tailors in Kenya.

To Nickson Karia, who is figuring out a way for banking customers to contribute a portion of their loyalty points towards the humanitarian projects they care about most.

To Onyancha Chrispinus, who is creating a secure, affordable and convenient healthcare microsaving and credit line for underserved Ugandans.

To Peter Akech, who is seeking to help patients track their prescription history through a digital platform.

To Peter Njeri aka Mr Garbage, turning garbage into cooking oil.

Ronald Sebuhinja, who is creating a more convenient digital way of managing information and processes for educators

To Rosine Mwiseneza, who is solving the water shortage on farms in Rwanda with IOT.

To Wilson Mnyabwilo, who provides up-to-date information on the academic progress of their children better than going in-person to school through a mobile application in Uganda

To the founders of Equilo and StorkCard:

To Rachel Elsinga and Jessica Menon. Thank you for putting aside the safe jobs and chasing after making equality in the world a real thing.

To Andres Korin and Bruce Pannaman for seeking to leverage your own experiences to help other new families in the London area. Your service is SO needed.

We love you all. You've changed the course of our lives in ways we never could have imagined.

Thank you,
Jeremiah and Dona